Enforcing
Air Pollution Controls

Esther Roditti Schachter

Published in cooperation with
the Center for Policy Research

The Praeger Special Studies program—
utilizing the most modern and efficient book
production techniques and a selective
worldwide distribution network—makes
available to the academic, government, and
business communities significant, timely
research in U.S. and international economic, social, and political development.

Enforcing
Air Pollution Controls
Case Study of
New York City

Praeger Publishers   New York   Washington   London

Library of Congress Cataloging in Publication Data

Schachter, Esther Roditti.
    Enforcing air pollution controls.

    (Praeger special studies in U.S. economic,
social, and political issues)
    Includes bibliographical references.
    1. Air—Pollution—Law and legislation—
New York (City)   I. Title.
KFX2048. S3   344'. 7471'0463   73-8165

PRAEGER PUBLISHERS
111 Fourth Avenue, New York, N.Y. 10003, U.S.A.
5, Cromwell Place, London SW7 2JL, England

Published in the United States of America in 1974
by Praeger Publishers, Inc.

Printed in the United States of America

This book was prepared under a grant by
the Ford Foundation to the Center for
Policy Research, New York City

To Oscar, Charles, and Susan

A surprising number of people, both citizens and community
leaders, still tend to assume, implicitly at least, that if you pass a
law you achieve a desired social change. Hence, the frequent call to
outlaw this or that (say, pollution) or to bring into being a desired
goal (say, eliminate poverty or desegregate schools).

But the record shows that while a law is a societal tool, its impact
is often much, much smaller than its advocates—and its opponents—
expect.

The reasons for this basic weakness of the law are many. We
are only beginning to understand the processes through which societies
can be deliberately changed, the complex forces of societal resistance
to change, and the rare occasions when societies open up and allow
massive transformations.

Viewed in this context, Esther Roditti Schacter's valuable volume
is a study in why laws are not enforced—and also, under what conditions they could be effective. The study deals with many aspects of
this issue and zeroes in on a critical point: the features of those who
must make the law work, a vital link in the chain that leads from enactment of a law to a change in society.

The law is, at least initially, just a piece of paper. Polluters
will not stop polluting, or embark on costly modification of their factories, or otherwise change because a group of legislators in Albany
or Washington, or both, raise their hands in affirmation of an abstract
idea. Even if polluters are watched by ever vigilant people, many
other things must happen, under most circumstances, before a law
"takes."

The fine volume before the reader is a meticulous study of this
process. No one interested in the way societies operate or change,
or in the ways laws work or fail, can afford to overlook its findings.

The study is part of a larger effort by legal talent, social scien-
tists, engineers, and members of a dozen other disciplines to work
out the conditions under which society can be more effectively and
responsibly managed by its members, a work in progress under the
auspices of the Center for Policy Research.

Amitai Etzioni

CONTENTS

LIST OF TABLES

The most serious problem facing environmentalists today is the enforcement of air and other pollution control laws. That is the concern, of this book, which uses New York City's air pollution control laws and practices as a case study.

New York uniquely qualifies as an example. Its air pollution control laws are among the country's toughest and oldest (they date from 1899). New York also has the longest air pollution enforcement history in the nation, with bureaucratic efforts going back to the 1930s. Yet it has been the most polluted city in the country, its air containing every known pollutant in quantities ranging from unhealthy to dangerous.

Much can be learned from New York City's efforts, and so the primary thrust of this study is the analysis, in concrete terms, of New York's laws and enforcement practices: What air pollution controls have been enacted? Are the laws enforced, and how? Have the laws had any impact?

Suggestions for change are based on an examination of laws that have worked and laws that have not, that is, the enforcement feasibility of individual components of the air pollution control code.

Failure to consider the law's enforcement feasibility has resulted in considerable wasted effort and resources. In repeatedly revising New York City's air pollution control laws, city officials considered economic, political, and technical feasibility while generally ignoring enforcement feasibility—despite the fact that a show of coercion is the principal means of attaining cleaner air. The basic goal of pollution enforcement is to change the behavior of individuals and organizations—including governmental bodies—by forcing compliance with the law. Voluntary compliance is unusual, and for good reason: It is inconvenient, it oftens requires substantial system changes, and in the short run it may be uneconomic.

Air pollution laws can no longer afford to ignore these obstacles. Laws must be tough, but a reasonable expectation of enforceability by the responsible jurisdiction must be inherent in their design.

Air pollution control laws traditionally have been enforced by inspectors charged with policing every pollution source in the community. But no local or state governmental body can ever reasonably expect to accomplish such a goal, and in any case this does not seem a socially desirable expenditure of resources: Most urban communities have too many pollution sources. Some, but not all, sources can be policed; those that can be eliminated must be eliminated, and others must be dealt with by law, at an earlier point than the emission of pollution from a stack.

I believe local laws can and should play a decisive role in bringing about cleaner air. Direct federal enforcement will not be necessary if New York City, and other local and state governments, treat the problem of enforcing air pollution control laws as seriously, realistically, and courageously as they have treated the substantive aspect of the law. Tough but unenforcable laws are useless, except to temporarily placate the public with the illusion that someone is doing something about pollution. Meanwhile, air pollution levels remain unhealthy. We haven't much time left to restore the air to the minimum federal standards required by 1975. We need tough and enforceable laws.

Enforcing
Air Pollution Controls

"N.Y.C. enacts toughest air pollution control code in the country."
In recent years such headline-making statements by Mayor
John V. Lindsay have appeared on the front pages of New York news-
papers. Is the statement true? On the one hand, yes, because New
York is probably a world leader with respect to its air pollution
control standards—although a leader only in comparison to the standards of other communities, not in comparison to the severity of its
own air pollution problem. But, on the other hand, New York does not
have the power to enforce its tough standards. (Power is here used
to mean both the Air Resources Department's legal powers as delegated
to it by the City Council, and the city government's resources and
ability to effectuate its public policy.)

This chapter describes the city's air pollution control laws and
indicates whether particular provisions are enforced by the Air

---

This study was completed in January 1972, just about the time
that a newly amended New York City air pollution control law became effective. However, the substantive changes in the new law do
not affect the conclusions of this study. The new law did create the
first administrative remedies—a newly created Environmental Control
Board with power to enforce the law and impose penalties. Unfortunately, no such board had been appointed by Feb. 1973 and therefore
administrative enforcement cannot be properly evaluated. Criminal
court proceedings continue to be the actual enforcement technique.

For a broader and more analytic discussion of the enforcement
of state and local air pollution control laws see Esther Roditti Schachter,
"Some Criteria for Evaluating State and Local Air Pollution Control
Laws," Boston College Commercial and Industrial Law Review, spring
1973.

Resources Department. The purpose of going through this sort of checklist is to establish exactly what the laws are (and, by inference, what the laws are not); to determine exactly which of the many laws are enforced; and to acquire some notion of the manner and degree to which the "enforced" laws actually are enforced.[1]

While reviewing the air pollution control laws, it is well to consider whether stiff standards—standards restricting the amount of pollutants emitted or the amount of pollutants contained in a fuel, or requiring strict upgrading of polluting equipment—can, in and of themselves, ever solve the city's air pollution control problem, or whether it is necessary to restrict pollution sources and even energy sources. To date the first approach has been the primary thrust of enforcement in New York City. But, as we shall see, it has not been possible to enforce the many air pollution control laws or control the vast number of emission sources, because of a variety of problems; thus, it is necessary to reconsider the very basic question of approach..

The oldest air pollution control law in the city forbids the emission of smoke, except for very limited time periods.[2] The bulk of the 40,000 annual citizen complaints concern smoke (see Table A.3).[3] Does the Department enforce this law? Yes, to the extent of its available resources. The records available indicate this has been the most thoroughly enforced air pollution control law.[4]

The smoke emission law, which has been on the city books for about 75 years, was intermittently enforced at first and has been consistently enforced during the past twenty years.[5] This kind of law is not only old, it is common. Every jurisdiction with an air pollution control law of any sort prohibits or restricts the emission of smoke. (During the late nineteenth century most major industrial cities enacted smoke control ordinances: Chicago in April 1881, Cincinnati in November 1881, St. Louis in 1893. These cities' ordinances were no more successful than that in New York.) In the New York metropolitan area, other jurisdictions with smoke emission laws include New York State, Nassau and Westchester counties, New Jersey, and many of New Jersey cities and counties bordering New York.[6]

But New York City has the broadest and strictest smoke law in the metropolitan area. It even prohibits smoke from coming into New York across the Hudson River or other jurisdictional boundaries— a potentially useful provision that has never been enforced.[7]

Emissions From Motor Vehicles and
Construction Equipment

New York City prohibits the emission of visible air contaminants from internal combustion engines, except for a very limited period. This includes autos, buses, trucks, construction equipment—anything

2

powered by an internal combustion engine. (In the fall of 1971 New York City amended its code to include external combustion engines as well as "internal" ones.) New York State and New Jersey's prohibition applies only to diesel-powered motor vehicles.[8]

Does the Department enforce this law? "Sporadically," according to Alfred Pieratti, the Department's executive director of engineering and enforcement. He said:

> There have been drives, periods of concentration. . . .
> The drives usually last a week. During that time I pull
> my men off other jobs and we concentrate—like, we do
> nothing but station people near the bridges. . . . It makes
> good press release for the politicians. . . .
>   Of course, we pick up emissions all the time when
> we see them. There is no pattern to these drives. The
> commissioner or deputy decides something is of first
> priority, that right now we should drop everything to do
> this drive. We don't have enough people to do an effec-
> tive job in any category. So we take a patch off one point
> and put it on another point.[9]

Despite this comment, and the number of violations the most casual city stroller observes, the record shows that only 352 summonses were issued for motor vehicle violations in 1968, and only 69 in 1969. The records show no entry for construction equipment, except possibly under "miscellaneous," which covers an average total of 150 to 200 summonses annually. A monthly breakdown for a recent year illustrates a typical pattern of enforcement "drives." Six motor vehicle summonses were issued in January 1969, none in February and March, one in April, five in May, three in June, four in July, two in August, five in September, twenty-five in October, eleven in November, and seven in December.

Licensing of Construction Equipment

Portable and stationary equipment using an internal combustion engine in the same location for ten days or more is supposed to have an operating certificate from the Department.[10] Do users of such equipment obtain the required certificates? Pieratti doubted it, and judging from the activities of the Department, and lacking any data to support enforcement, this law will be classified as not enforced.

Sulfur Dioxide Emissions in Manufacturing

New York City prohibits the emission of sulfur dioxide from manufacturing equipment in excess of specified standards, and requires

manufacturing industries to obtain operating certificates.11 The law
has never been enforced because there are no industries emitting
sulfur in the course of manufacturing in New York City. According
to Pieratti, "The law may be preventive. I once got a call from a guy
who wanted to open such an establishment. He never did, so maybe
the rule discouraged him."12

Particulate Emission

The law restricts the emission of particulates on a weight-rated
basis.13 Pieratti said:

> The principal purpose of this rule is to control industry
> because its emissions may not be visible. It's not used
> for boilers or incinerators. If you can see something,
> you don't need to worry about weight-rate, because you
> can get them with a Ringelmann rating*. . . . Used the
> rule? I remember we used it prior to '64 when visible
> emissions were less tight, and we used it at least once
> in '64 or '65. Also used it to test a prototype incinera-
> tor. What's happening now is that we are playing around
> with industrial processes. No one ever gave us the man-
> power to identify industrial processes and know what's
> going on. Now that the state has required each industry
> to self-report we may use this rule. . . . No, we don't
> stack-test—it's very expensive. [Estimated cost is
> $3-4,000 per stack.]14

This law, then, is not enforced.

General Health and Odors

The law prohibits any emission, including odors and water vapor,
that may harm the health, welfare, or comfort of any person, property,
or business. It also prohibits any emission that may not be harmful
in itself but may cause harm if it reacts with other elements in the
air, including sunlight, to produce a harmful solid, liquid, or gas,
e.g., photochemical smog.15 This broad provision has been the law
in New York City since 1964. Prior to that time a similar but more
restrictive "nuisance" provision empowered the department to act in
case of harm to the public health. The older nuisance provision was
principally used in cases of odors. Is the present provision enforced?

———————————————

*The Ringelmann chart measures darkness and opacity of smoke.

I was told it is,[16] but I suspect it is not generally enforced except with respect to odors, and then only infrequently.

Airborne Particulates

The law requires that materials prone to causing particulate matter to become airborne shall be handled, transported, and stored in a manner that prevents their becoming airborne, that construction and demolition be done in a similar manner, and that untreated open areas in manufacturing districts be maintained in a similar manner.[17]

This law was not enforced until 1969, when the Department decided to take action to control the spraying of asbestos at construction sites throughout the city. Asbestos is a known serious health hazard that may cause mesothelioma, a form of incurable lung cancer, and other cancers. In late 1969 the World Trade Center was about to be sprayed, and because of the building's unusual height, it was feared that the entire city might undergo an "asbestos snow." The Department acted and the World Trade Center spraying was prevented. Other asbestos spraying also was somewhat restricted.[18]

Agency enforcement of asbestos spraying will be discussed in detail in a separate case study. For now, it should be noted that the asbestos spraying action is the only time this section has been enforced. Statements by two experts indicate some of the reasons for enforcing this important law. Harold Romer, assistant commissioner of the Air Resources Department, said:

> Demolition dust, including old asbestos, is a serious source of air pollution. Did you know that in 1968 about 4,000 buildings were demolished in the city? The same for 1969, and we anticipate a 25 to 30 percent increase of that figure if proposed housing programs go ahead. The dust is so bad that you can sometimes get #3 or #4 Ringelmann readings [the equivalent of black smoke] from the dust."[19]

Dr. Irving Selikoff, a specialist in environmental medicine, told the New York City Council that asbestos in the air in quantities greater than an occasional nonhazardous fiber is caused by a few specific uses: (1) factory emissions (one known factory in New York City), (2) transportation of asbestos material (a serious New York City health hazard), (3) warehousing of asbestos (also serious in New York City), and (4) use of asbestos in construction (also serious in New York City).[20]

Equipment Operation and Maintenance

The law requires proper maintenance and use of equipment emitting air contaminants.[21] This is a critical section because badly operated or maintained equipment will smoke even if it was originally high-quality, nonsmoking equipment. Improper maintenance and operation is undoubtedly a major cause of air pollution, a fact that will probably become apparent to New York residents a few years after the upgrading of incinerators and boilers in the city has been completed. In fact, proper maintenance and operation is the major chink in the armor of law enforcement. It requires the impossible—continuous surveillance of hundreds of thousands of pieces of equipment. It is not in the economic self-interest of an owner to maintain and operate his equipment to the degree necessary to avoid smoke.

Pieratti said the section is enforced: "We issue violation notices [informal warnings] on this all the time. Problem is followup—don't have enough inspectors to do reinspections in all cases. If they don't comply, they get a summons."[22] (It has never been satisfactorily explained why summonses are not issued in the first instance: A summons would avoid reinspection, and if the fine were high enough to make it cheaper to repair, a summons also would avoid excessive repeat violators.)

The available statistics show no separate entry for equipment violations—they are grouped with Local Law 14 upgrading violations.* During one month, January 1970, a breakdown was made: of a total of 162 summonses, 136 were for failure to upgrade and 25 were for defective equipment.

The law also prohibits the operation of equipment fitted with air pollution control apparatus unless the control apparatus is used.[23] Is the law enforced? Yes, in the same manner and to about the degree as the equipment maintenance law.[24] The purpose of the law is to prevent an owner or operator from disconnecting the smoke alarm or the combustion shutoff—a not uncommon practice.

The law also regulates the proper use of air contaminant detectors, combustion shutoffs, and air contaminant recorders.[25] Is the law enforced? According to Pieratti, Yes, about the same as the other equipment sections.[26]

Licensed Supervision

The law requires that manual oil burners be supervised by a licensed person.[27] Pieratti did not even recall this section; we had

---

*Local Law 14 involves amendments to the New York City Administrative Law relating to air pollution control enacted by the City Council in 1966 and 1969 under the leadership of Robert Low, former councilman and chairman of the Special Committee to Investigate Air Pollution.

to look it up. Then he said, "It is not used because oil burning operations are 99.9 percent automatic."28

Incinerator Operator Hours

The law prohibits the operation of incinerators except between
the hours of 7:00 a.m. and 5:00 p.m.29 Is the law enforced? "No,"
Pieratti said. "A nice rule, but we don't have inspectors except between 8:00 a.m. and 4:00 p.m."30

Motor Vehicle Idling

The law prohibits a motor vehicle (including buses, trucks, and
chauffeured limousines) from idling for more than 3 minutes.31 "We
all know that law isn't enforced," Pieratti said. "We enforce when
we see it, or during an occasional enforcement drive. We had a one-
week drive just before Christmas."32

Soot Blowing

The law prohibits "soot blowing" by vessels in New York City's
harbors.33 Soot blowing is a procedure for cleaning boiler tubes by
blasting air through the tubes, dislodging the soot, and blowing it out
into the open air. The boiler tubes must be regularly cleaned for
proper maintenance and avoidance of continuous smoke. Soot blowing
is the oldest, cheapest, and most common cleaning procedure. According to former Air Resources Commissioner Robert N. Rickles,
less air pollution is caused by allowing soot blowing than by prohibiting
it.34 But ships can blow their stacks at sea rather than in the harbor.
Is the rule enforced? "No," Pieratti said, "I don't know how often it
occurs. I haven't got the personnel to study it."35
Interviews with citizen groups brought up complaints about soot
blowing by the New York State Housing Authority.36 When asked about
this, Pieratti said, "It's not against the law, except for ships. The
Code allows soot blowing if it's done in a manner that's invisible,
which is possible to do."37 Yet invisible particulates are the most
dangerous to health because they are small enough to be inhaled into
the deepest recesses of the lungs.

Sulfur Content of Fuel

The law prohibits the use of certain kinds or grades of fuel, and
the burning of refuse in fuel-burning equipment not designed for it.38
(Refuse could be used as fuel in the right kind of equipment.) "Such
shenanigans do occur, and we pick it up occasionally," Pieratti said.39

The law also restricts the sulfur content of residual and other fuel oils.[40] The sulfur released from fuel oils and coal during combustion is the major source of a serious New York City air pollutant— sulfur dioxide. In fact New York City has one of the highest concentrations of sulfur dioxide in the country. Combined with particulates, which New York also has in quantity, sulfur dioxide is a well-established killer. The London smog of 1952, which contained substantial quantities of sulfur dioxide and particulates, killed 4,000 persons.

This law is enforced. In fact it is unique because it is the only air pollution control law in New York City that is easy to enforce, and that is complied with, despite strong initial protest. However, enforcement and compliance have had only a limited impact on New York City's air. The citywide average of sulfur dioxide is lower, but the amount continues at dangerous levels. In addition, the sulfur dioxide levels in Queens and Staten Island went up in 1970, and the experts are not entirely sure why. They suspect the wind "blew the stuff over there."[41]

To aid enforcement of the fuel sulfur restrictions, the law requires the maintenance of specified records, fuel information tickets, and delivery tickets.[42] Pieratti said these records are spot-checked and little discrepancy is found.[43]

Volatile Content of Coal

The law restricts the volatile content of solid fuels.[44] This restriction applies only to bituminous or soft coal; the other major type of coal, anthracite or hard coal, naturally contains a low volatile content. Bituminous coal is heavily used because it is cheaper than anthracite. Why is high volatile content a problem? Pieratti said:

Well, it's tricky to use without causing smoke which contains gases. Until the heat is up, it smokes. Theoretically, once it's properly started it won't smoke. . . . However, coal burners are manually operated, and are never properly operated on a daily basis. . . . You are beating a dead horse because they will always push the boiler before it is ready to go . . . and maintenance is usually neglected because of the need of the men to do other work. As long as the boiler works, what does he care?"[45]

In addition, using coal in small boilers, which cannot be fitted with expensive control equipment, will cause the emission of excessive particulates.

8

This section of the law is not enforced, Pieratti said, because another section of the law, enacted in the spring of 1971, two years later, outlawed the use of bituminous coal for heat and hot water (but not for power generation).[46] However, in 1966 the Lindsay administration privately consented to the use of bituminous coal by about 600 to 1,000 private users. The department does not know exactly how many private users there are in the city. Pieratti thinks coal burning "will naturally peter out because it's difficult to get the superintendent to carry out the ashes . . . and that between 1966 and '71 an estimated 70,000 tons of soft coal was replaced by natural gas." (Underscore mine—no one really knows the figure.)[47]

Why did the Lindsay administration consent to the continued use of an outlawed fuel? In 1969 several coal distributors, and some Brooklyn and Queens landlords, sued New York City, John Lindsay, Dr. Merrill Eisenbud, (then administrator of the Environment Protection Administration), and Austin Heller, (then commissioner of Air Pollution Control), complaining that the outlawing of bituminous coal was unconstitutional, and that the coal they used satisfied the code standards on smoke, particulate, and volatile emission. In addition, the coal contained 0.6 percent sulfur, satisfying the sulfur-in-fuel standards. Affidavits were submitted by two experts, one of whom was Aaron J. Teller (a well known industrial consultant and former dean of Cooper Union). Apparently, the problem was that, although the plaintiffs were theoretically right on all counts, as a practical matter the equipment would emit excessive smoke and particulate matter because of faulty operating and maintenance practices. But the sulfur content of the fuel is not affected by operation or maintenance. The city was at that time engaged in another major court battle challenging the constitutionality of its air pollution control laws. It clearly was not anxious to take on a second battle.[48] In addition, the focus of attention at the time was to cut down the amount of sulfur, and the use of bituminous coal would not adversely affect that goal. It also was assumed that the use of coal burners would naturally die out. So the city consented to the use of the illegal fuel. According to Pieratti,

> Inspectors were sent out just before the agreement to
> pick up smoke violations on some of these burners, based
> on a customer list supplied by the Coal Trade Association,
> and there were none. Nobody knows the exact number of
> coal burners used in the city today. From time to time
> I send inspectors out on the basis of the 1969 customer
> list, which we know represents maybe one-half or one-
> third of the total customers.[49]

Here it is appropriate to make a note about the legal use of bituminous coal by Consolidated Edison. In 1970 it was still using about 2.5 million tons a year with a 99 percent effective electrostatic precipitation. Theoretically the equipment would therefore emit only 1 percent of the particulates caused by the combustion of 2.5 million tons of coal—about 2,900 pounds in 1970.[50] But, Pieratti said, "Again the problem is operational and maintenance. All Con Ed has to do is to keep the equipment working properly. Did you know that last year it came out before the State Public Service Commission that Con Ed has insufficient maintenance crews? Also, during the normal course of operation they sometimes must push a boiler too fast, and it smokes badly."[51]

Summertime Use of Fuel Oil

The law strictly restricts the summertime use of residual fuel oil (number 6) because sulfur dioxide mixed with particulates is more dangerous in hot humid weather than in cold weather.[52] Also, summertime restrictions theoretically should be easier to comply with because much less fuel is consumed than during the winter. (In summer the fuel is used solely for hot water.)

Is the law enforced? "No," Pieratti said, "because if the equipment is upgraded as required by another section enacted in 1966, two years after this section, then this section is irrelevant. We do enforce indirectly by concentrating on upgrading."[53] Meanwhile, most boilers have not been upgraded and the summertime restrictions have not been enforced for seven years.

Upgrading Equipment

The law requires the upgrading of private and public fuel burning and refuse burning equipment (boilers and incinerators). As an alternative, incinerators in very small buildings may be shut down, and in larger buildings the owner may, if he wishes, install a refuse compactor. The law specifies the particular type of equipment that must be installed in order to legally upgrade, with the exception of municipal incinerators, which are prohibited from operating without the installation and use of "control apparatus which incorporates the most effective advances in the art of air pollution control as determined by the Commissioner."[54]

These sections of the law were enacted in 1966 (upgrading requirements) and 1968 (optional closedown and refuse compactor). Is the law enforced? While according to then Commissioner Rickles, in 1971, "approximately 60 percent of our staff of 260 continues to be devoted to enforcement of upgrading laws,"[55] 60 percent or more of private and public owners had not complied at that time. Compliance figures show that, as of August 1971, only 15 percent of the incinerators

10

operated by the New York City Board of Education, Hospital Corporation, and Housing Authority were upgraded or discontinued in compliance with the 1966 law (figures are not available on compliance by other governmental bodies). As of January 1, 1972, about 29 percent of privately operated incinerators were upgraded or discontinued. As of August 1971, 41 percent of the oil burners operated by the Board of Education, Hospital Corporation, and Housing Authority had complied, while as of January 1, 1972, about 27 percent of private oil burners had complied.[56]

The provisions applicable to municipal incinerators are not enforced. "We can't really," Pieratti said. "We are all under the same boss now. [Air Pollution Control and Sanitation are subdivisions of the Environmental Protection Administration.] We used to write up violation notices [informal warnings] on city incinerators and send them to Sanitation, but with the same boss the system is cockeyed."[57] (However, the effectiveness of past practices is clearly questionable since municipal incinerators were and continue to be in poor working condition.)

These sections of the law were the subject of a major legal controversy (Oriental Boulevard Co. vs. Heller). The city won the case in December 1970 after four years of litigation. They continue to be the most controversial and politically sensitive sections of the law and the history of their enforcement is very complex. The upgrading provision will therefore be discussed in more detail in a separate chapter.

Outlawing of Private Incinerators

In 1966 the law prohibited the installation of private incinerators in New York City as of May 1968. Instead, new buildings are required to install refuse compactors.[58] Is the law enforced? According to a confidential communication,

> "No . . . no way to check on illegally installed incinerators, unless they happen to smoke. How do we know if someone puts in an incinerator unless they file for a permit? I know of one illegal installation—there may be more. The _____ Company filed an application to install a new, bigger incinerator and we (i.e., the department) refused the permit because it is prohibited by law. Someone above the commissioner's level said to give him the permit, the orders came down, so they were allowed to go ahead. We do what we are supposed to do, we wanted to refuse the permit. . . . Yes, the incinerator is operating now."[59]

TABLE 1

Summary of Control Enforcement

Control	Level of Enforcement
Smoke emission	High
Emissions from motor vehicles	Low
Emissions from construction equipment	No activity
Sulfur dioxide from manufacturing equipment	No activity
Particulate emission weight-rate standard	Low
General health and odors	Low
Airborne particulates:	
Asbestos	High
Other particulates	No activity
Equipment and control apparatus operation and maintenance laws	Low
Licensed supervisor	No activity
Incinerator operation between 7:00 a.m. and 5:00 p.m.	No activity
Idling for more than three minutes	No activity
Soot blowing by ships	No activity
Sulfur content of fuel and required records	High
Volatile content of coal	No activity
Bituminous coal outlawed	No activity
Summertime use of residual oil	No activity
Upgrading of boilers and incinerators	High
Upgrading of municipal incinerators	No activity
Private incinerators outlawed	No activity
Certification of fuel burner and incinerator operators and supervisors	Low

The department does not systematically check new buildings to be sure that compactors, not incinerators, are installed.

Certification of Operators and Supervisors

The law requires operators and supervisors of residual fuel burning and refuse burning equipment to attend a school in order to learn proper operating and maintenance procedures.[60] At the end of the course they receive a certificate from the city. A boiler or incinerator is not supposed to be operated or supervised by anyone who does not hold a certificate.

Is the law enforced? According to Pieratti,

Well, it's known that most operators don't have certificates. We ask for them when we check the equipment out. . . . How many? My guess is that 40,000 out of 50,000 don't have the certificate. We issue violation notices [informal warnings] if there is no certificate, not summonses. It's usually not the guy's fault. We don't give many classes, and for those who speak only Spanish, we have only one class in the Bronx.[61]

Also, the men are not paid to come to class, and there is no other incentive for coming. On the contrary, the men lose time and carfare if they comply, and many who hold two or three jobs do not have the time or money. The notion behind the law, improving operation and maintenance, was fine, but it failed to consider attendance and application incentives. Even if the operator attends the course and obtains a certificate, there is no incentive for him to properly operate and maintain the equipment. He is not likely to be caught, the equipment will work anyway, and most owners do not want high maintenance or operation costs. As it stands, the law is unlikely to work.

Table 1 may be useful as a summary and rough gauge of department activity. The category enforcement activity "incorporates the issuance of violation notices (informal warnings) and summonses which never reach the court, as well as writ activity. It should be noted however that agency activity does not necessarily result in compliance. Only the categories of "high" and "low" activity are used because data is unavailable for a more refined degree of reporting.

NOTES

1. My information as to whether a law is enforced is based on the only available sources: interviews and two intradepartmental

memos that show the number of summonses served, according to type of violation, for 1968 and 1969. These two memos show the following cases scheduled for court action or summons study:

	Smoke Emission	Motor Vehicle	Local Law 14 and Other
1968	1,636	352	690
1969	1,464	69	2,989

The month of January 1970 is covered in somewhat more detail: 302 smoke emission cases, 3 motor vehicle cases, 136 under Local Law 14, 17 for defective equipment, 6 for defective smoke alarm, one for operating certificate, and 2 for defective smoke detector.

It should be noted that service of a summons does not mean court enforcement nor compliance with the law. The case may not have been prosecuted (for example, the Department may withdraw a summons), if the case got to court it may not have been heard (thousands of court cases were outstanding), and if heard, the case may have been dismissed or appealed. On the other hand, the absence of summons service does not mean that a law is not informally enforced and complied with, as on sulfur limitation in fuel.

2. See Sanitary Code, sec. 134 (1899), since amended; N.Y.C. Air Administration Code, ch. 57, sec. 1403.2-9.03 (Supp. 1971).

3. The commonly quoted figure is 40,000, but Department statistics on citizen complaints show the number received in recent years to be 5-10,000 fewer.

4. Interview with Pieratti, April 12, 1971; intradepartmental memos entitled Cases Scheduled for Court Action, Summons Study undated and reported in footnote 1.

5. Sanitary Code, sec. 134 (1898); Pieratti, April 12, 1971.

6. 10 N.Y. Codes, Rules and Regulations, sec. 191.2 (1969); Nassau County, N.Y., Adm. Code, sec. 9-21.42; Westchester County Sanitary Code, art. 16, sec. 1614 (1971); N.J. Air Pollution Control Code, ch. 4, sec. 2.1, e.g. East Orange, Ordinance no. 12, sec 4 (1964), N.J., Ordinance no. 65A, sec. 5 (1958).

7. N.Y.C. Air Administration Code, ch. 57, sec. 9.03 (b) (2) (Supp. 1971).

8. N.Y.C. Admin. Code, ch. 57, sec. 1403. 2-9.05, (1971); 10 N.Y. Codes, Rules and Regs., sec. 193; N.J. Air Pollution Control Code, ch. 14, sec. 2.

9. Pieratti, April 12, 1971. See also footnote 1.

10. N.Y.C. Adm. Code, ch. 41, sec. 892-4.5 (this section was enacted in 1966 and repealed in 1971).

11. N.Y.C. Adm. Code, ch. 57, sec. 1403.2-9.07 (1971).

12. Pieratti, April 12, 1971.

13. N.Y.C. Adm. Code, ch. 57, sec. 1403.2-9.09 (1971).

14. Pieratti, April 12, 1971. The estimated cost of stack-testing was made by former Commissioner Rickles at the executive session of the Environmental Protection Committee of New York City Council on May 7, 1971.

15. N.Y.C. Adm. Code, ch. 47, sec. 1403.2-9.01 (1971).

16. Pieratti, April 12, 1971.

17. N.Y.C. Adm. Code, ch. 57, sec. 1403.2-9.11 (1971). Note that at the time the law was enforced to control asbestos spraying, the law referred generally to airborne particulate matter without explicit reference to asbestos: see N.Y.C. Adm. Code, ch. 41, sec. 9.15 (repealed 1971).

18. Interviews Kramer 4/9/71 and Fabricant 11/70.

19. Interview with Romer, January 1, 1971.

20. Testimony of Dr. Irving J. Selikoff, chief of the Division of Environmental Medicine, City University, Mt. Sinai School of Medicine, to the executive session of the New York City Council, Committee on Environmental Protection, February 25, 1971.

21. N.Y.C. Adm. Code, ch. 57, sec. 1403.2-11.01 (1971).

22. Pieratti, April 12, 1971. The backlog of inspections for 1970 numbered 12,000 according to an untitled intradepartmental report, of March 1971.

23. N.Y.C. Adm. Code, ch. 57, sec. 1403.2-11.03 (1971).

24. Pieratti, April 12, 1971.

25. N.Y.C. Adm. Code, ch. 57, sec. 1403.2-11.19, 11.21 and 11.23 (1971).

26. Pieratti, April 12, 1971.

27. N.Y.C. Adm. Code, ch. 57, sec. 1403.2-11.09 (1971).

28. Pieratti, April 12, 1971.

29. N.Y.C. Adm. Code, ch. 57, sec. 1403.2-11.13 (1971).

30. Pieratti, April 12, 1971.

31. N.Y.C. Adm. Code, ch. 57, sec. 1403.2-11.15 (1971).

32. Pieratti, April 12, 1971.

33. N.Y.C. Adm. Code, ch. 57, sec. 1403.2-11.17 (1971).

34. Testimony of former Commissioner Robert Rickles at an executive session of the New York City Council, Committee on Environmental Protection, April 30, 1971.

35. Pieratti, April 12, 1971.

36. For example, interview with Kenneth Kowald, former executive secretary, N.Y. State Action for Clean Air Committee, spring 1971.

37. Pieratti, April 12, 1971.

38. N.Y.C. Air Pollution Control Code, sec. 1301. Section was repealed in 1971.

39. Pieratti, April 12, 1971.
40. N.Y.C. Adm. Code, ch. 57, sec. 14.03.2-13.03 13.03 (1971).
41. Interview with Ferrand, April 21, 1971.
42. N.Y.C. Adm. Code, ch. 57, sec. 1403.2-13.13 and 13.15 (1971).
43. Pieratti, April 21, 1971.
44. N.Y.C. Adm. Code, ch. 57, sec. 1403.2-13.07 (1971).
45. Pieratti, April 12, 1971. A note of historical interest: The first New York City air pollution control law, a Brooklyn ordinance of 1895, forbade the use of soft coal in factories, engine rooms, or electric stations within a 4-mile radius of City Hall.
46. N.Y.C. Adm. Code, ch. 41, sec. 893-2.0, amended ch. 57, sec. 1403.2-13.01 (c), which legalizes the use of coal at the discretion of the Environmental Protection Administration under specified conditions.
47. Pieratti, April 12, 1971.
48. The coal distributors' case is Plymouth Rock Fuel Corp. v The City of New York, Supreme Court, New York County (1969). Suit filed and settled out of court; the other simultaneous case is Oriental Boulevard Co. v. Heller, 27 N.Y. 2d 212, 265 N.E. 2d Ct. of Appeals N.Y. (1970).
49. Pieratti, April 12, 1971.
50. Intradepartmental Quarterly Progress Report, Emission Inventory, December 31, 1970, under the heading "Con Ed," an unpaginated sheet entitled "Fuel Consumption and Emission Inventory of Con Edison Power Plants for Year Beginning January 1970 and ending December 31, 1970."
51. Pieratti, April 12, 1971.
52. N.Y.C. Air Pollution Control Code, sec. 1307 (1964). Section was repealed in 1971.
53. Pieratti, April 12, 1971.
54. N.Y.C. Adm. Code, ch. 57, sec. 1403.2-4.01 (1971; N.Y.C. Adm Code, ch. 41, sec. 892-4.3, 893-3.0, and 893-4.0 (1966), amended, ch. 57, sec. 1403.2-4.01-4.05 (1971); N.Y.C. Adm. Code, ch. 41, sec. 892-4.2 (1966), amended ch. 57, sec. 1403.2-5.05 (b) (2) (1971).
55. Letter to The New York Times, April 24, 1971, from Commissioner Robert Rickles. The staff figure indicates everyone in the department, including the commissioner himself.
56. Intradepartmental memo, "Bureau of Engineering, Local Law 14 Status, Public Sector" (August 1971); intradepartmental memo, "Bureau of Engineering, Local Law 49 (amended number of Local Law 14)" (January 1972). The January report does not contain statistics for the public sector.
57. Pieratti, April 12, 1971.

58. N.Y.C. Adm. Code, ch. 41, sec. 893-3.0 (1966), amended ch. 57, sec. 1403.2-4.03 (1971).

59. Confidential communication.

60. N.Y.C. Adm. Code, ch. 57, sec. 1403.2-11.11 (1971).

61. Pieratti, April 12, 1971.

2

ADMINISTRATIVE POWERS
AND THEIR USE

What are the Air Resources Department's administrative enforcement powers, and to what extent are they being used?

The Department has had licensing powers since 1950. It has the authority to require installation, alteration, and operating permits for any equipment capable of emitting air pollution.[1] Department regulations enacted in 1954 prohibited the construction, reconstruction, installation, or alteration of any equipment capable of emitting air pollution, with some minor exceptions. The regulations also contained rather detailed specification standards for incinerators.[2] Were these regulations enforced? Yes and no. If a permit was requested, the plans and specifications were checked, permission to proceed was granted, and the completed work was inspected to see that the equipment conformed to the plans and specifications. If the equipment conformed, an operating permit was issued. The engineer did not check out the performance of the equipment. (The same procedure is followed today.)

Councilman Katz once asked then Commissioner Rickles, "You don't even bother to find out if it actually pollutes?"

Rickles answered, "This is not an inspection of the actual condition of the equipment. . . . Do you want a performance test on each job? Do you know what that costs? Three to four thousand dollars a test depending. . ."[3]

If an individual does not voluntarily comply by requesting a permit, the Department does not have any routine spot-checking procedures. (About 75,000 to 100,000 pieces of equipment are involved and there are only about a dozen engineers; there used to be fewer.) "There is no way to know, unless we catch the equipment smoking."[4] An indication of the probable high degree of noncompliance with the law is the fact that most of the industrial establishments checked by the Department in 1971 after the state required industrial self-reporting were found not to have permits for their boilers or incinerators, let alone their industrial equipment. Another indicator may be the fact that incinerators all over the city smoke even though most were built after 1954, when the City Council required new buildings to contain an incinerator. They may smoke because of poor operation and maintenance, or because of poor design. No one knows for certain.

In any event, the major drawbacks of the licensing provisions were (1) self-reporting was relied upon without adequate means of spot checking and (2) design standards were specified without checks on performance.

In 1964 the licensing provisions were extensively revised and the coverage broadened. Administrative procedures were established for the suspension or revocation of permits by the commissioner "for willful or continued violation of this code."[5] Conditional permit provisions were established, higher standards were approved, and so forth. However, enforcement procedures continued as before and the new provisions on conditional permits, suspensions, and revocations were not enforced.[6] "This is all cloud nine stuff," Pieratti said. "You are talking to a frustrated guy. When it gets up to the big guys, who would revoke [a permit]? They won't do it. Look, it just doesn't happen."[7]

In 1966 Local Law 14 further revised the licensing requirements. The principal change was to expand the permit requirement to cover not only new and altered equipment but also specified existing ("old") equipment, and to make operating permits valid for three years instead of forever. The equipment affected was existing fuel burning equipment, refuse burning equipment, manufacturing processes emitting sulfur, and portable equipment (used principally in construction.) The law prohibited the issuance of a permit for boilers and incinerators unless they were upgraded as specified in the law. Furthermore, operating permits can be revoked by the administrator and are renewable upon application to him.[8]

Is the law enforced? About 60 percent or more of the boilers and incinerators required to have a permit do not yet have one. No permits have been issued for portable equipment. Thus, the renewal provisions have not yet had a chance to operate. However, landlords have received oral assurances "that as long as the equipment is functioning we won't withdraw the operating certificate."[9] The reason for the assurance is to induce compliance with the upgrading provisions. It is understood that landlords and other owners will not make a $6-9,000 investment without assurances that the permit will in fact be valid for longer than three years.

Licensing provisions, in one form or another, have been operating in New York City for almost 20 years. It is eminently clear that the regulations are not working—either they are not enforced (self-reporting without systematic checking is unreliable) or they are not complied with when enforced (as in Local Law 14 upgrading permits).

To top it all, even when complied with, licensing without systematic reinspection does little to prevent the emission of air contaminants after the first few years when proper maintenance and repairs become important. The basic problem is that there are too many small pieces of equipment (or too few inspectors), and no incentive or self-interest to induce compliance. The equipment does its job for the owner whether or not it is polluting the air.

The Department was empowered in 1951 "to seal any equipment installed or operated without a permit . . . and [after notice and hearing] seal any equipment or prohibit any process responsible for the emission into the open air of harmful or objectionable substances."[10] In 1954 the administrative rules approved by the Department provided that three or more violations of the smoke emission law within a 12-month period could result in an administrative hearing and sealing. In 1964 the administrative rules, which became known as the Air Pollution Control Code, were tightened—two or more violations of any emission standard within a 12-month period could result in sealing. In addition, two new provisions were added: A polluting source could be sealed for the emission of a toxic air contaminant or for a single violation of an emission standard plus noncompliance with a commissioner's order.[11] In 1966 the sealing provisions were expanded. After January 1, 1965, boilers and incinerators operating without a Local Law 14 permit could be sealed and penalized.[12]

Is the law enforced? Until February 1971 not one piece of polluting equipment was sealed. In February the commissioner and his deputy appeared for the first sealing, and what occurred was most fitting:

> It was supposed to be a historic occasion—the first seal-
> ing. . . . But when a platoon of City officials and newsmen
> crowded into the tiny boiler room of a Brooklyn apartment
> building yesterday, the incinerator, alas, was gone. "How
> about that?" asked the Commissioner. "It was there
> yesterday," said the Deputy Commissioner. So they
> sealed a hole in the wall.[13]

Since that time there have been eleven sealings, all involving incinerators.[14]

Sealings were used as a threat for many years, although no data is available as to how effective such threats were. They also are used as a procedural device to get the pollutor in for an informal administrative hearing. "The trouble with the hearings is that you need clout to get compliance, and when we get compliance it's only from one person, which is no good. You need something better than one to one action."[15]

In addition to licensing and sealing powers, the administrator may "take such action as may be necessary to control the emission of air contamination which causes or may cause, by itself or in combination . . . detriment to the safety, health, welfare or comfort of the public, or to a part thereof, injury to plant or animal life, or damage to property or business." He may also "require alterations in any existing equipment or process for the purpose of processing compliance."[16]

These powers were exercised once. In the fall of 1970 quick action was needed to control the spraying of asbestos by the construction trades. Promulgation of formal rules by the Board of Air Pollution Control was considered too time-consuming, so the commissioner issued informal criteria requiring process alterations. This exercise of power was upheld by the court.[17] (In 1971 the City Council amended the section of the law empowering the Department to require alterations in order to obtain compliance by transferring that power to the N.Y.C. Environmental Control Board.[18])

The commissioner also may order equipment or fuel to be tested by the owner if he has reasonable cause to believe is in violation of the Code.[19] This power has never been exercised.[20]

The obvious theme running through the preceding discussion of administrative powers is that the City Council consistently delegated power without the resources to make it stick, and consistently underestimated the complexity of enforcing air pollution control laws. Even if the number of pollution sources were manageable, licensing provisions without adequate manpower are meaningless: The power to seal boilers is meaningless because the tenants will freeze in the winter and go without hot water in the summer. Power plants cannot be shut down. A limited number of incinerators can be sealed, if arrangements are made to pick up garbage. Industrial sealing has never been tried, but it would mean people thrown out of work. Administrative hearings are almost meaningless without the power to penalize. And repairs? There is no way to force the owner to repair unless a penalty exceeding the cost of the repair can be imposed expeditiously. When the administrator took the initiative and acted imaginatively and expeditiously, as in the case of asbestos spraying, the City Council Environmental Protective Committee (while considering air pollution control amendments) explicitly expressed its dissatisfaction and several members expressed private opinions doubting the legality of the action despite the court ruling. (The City Council in fact repealed the administrator's power to order alterations in order to attain compliance.)

The issue is whether the legislative body wants an effective administrative agency? The answer must be "No," because strict standards without resources and power are meaningless.

FIELD ENFORCEMENT STAFF

"They are a very fine group working against unbelievable ob- stacles . . . understaffed, low-paid, blamed for the lack of enforcement, physically isolated. Their morale is low and they have little commu- nication with management. Under the circumstances they do an amaz- ing job and with tremendous spirit."[21]

Harold Romer, assistant commissioner in charge of Planning and Administration, and former director of Field Services, so described the field enforcement staff. His statement accurately sums up long- standing problems of paramount importance to air pollution control inspectors and engineers. Underlying these problems are questions of resource allocation and status within the Air Resources Depart- ment. It is ironic that although inspection is the most important ele- ment in an enforcement program (the effectiveness of the present air pollution control law pivots around regular periodic inspections designed to detect and prevent violations), the inspectors, engineers, and their supervisors are at the bottom of the totem pole in pay and status.

Inspectors and engineers are part of Field Services, the Depart- ment's field enforcement arm. Field Services is divided into two groups: the Bureau of Engineering and the Bureau of Enforcement (inspectors). The former's job is to review all plans and specifica- tions required by law to be filed, and to inspect the equipment to be sure it conforms to the plans and specifications. The job of the latter group is to spot violations of the Air Pollution Control Code within New York City; to issue violation notices (informal warnings) and summonses in case of violations; to reinspect when violation notices are issued; to investigate citizen complaints and "mayor specials"; to manage, coordinate and appear at daily criminal court proceedings with respect to the prosecution of summonses; and to handle the necessary paperwork and statistical data.[22]

Alfred Pieratti directs Field Services. He is an engineer who has been with the Air Resources Department for about 10 years. Under Pieratti are three directors: Louis Leibowitz, an experienced private air pollution control engineer who has been with the agency about three years and heads the Enforcement Bureau (the inspectors); M. Saed, an engineer who has been with the Department for about six years and heads the Engineering Bureau; and Joseph Schechter, an accountant who has been with the Department about 6 years and heads the Bureau of Administration, which handles departmental statistics. The three bureau heads report to Pieratti, who in turn is responsible to Fred Hart, a deputy commissioner with a masters degree in engineering and business administration who has been with the Department about one year.23

The engineering and inspector groups were combined into one bureau in order to obtain "more coordinated activity as well as make possible closer supervision," according to a memo from Schechter. But the memo goes on to state that adequate supervision would require additional personnel as well as a full-time lawyer to supervise court personnel. Neither was expected to be provided in the foreseeable future.24

Coordination and supervision is further handicapped by the fact that the engineers and inspectors are not housed under the same roof, nor are they housed in the same building with the commissioner, his deputies, and other top management. The engineers are in the basement of a decrepit building at 41 Cooper Square, while the inspectors occupy two floors of an old building at 137 Centre Street. Pieratti, who maintains his office at 137 Centre Street, supervises the two groups by driving directly from his home to Cooper Square in the morning, remaining if there is a problem, and if not, going on to his office on Centre Street. Otherwise contact is by phone.25 The top executives and technical services are housed on two floors at Cooper Union in modern, carpeted, and air conditioned quarters. (The 137 Centre Street and 41 Cooper Square offices are old, uncarpeted, and cooled by fans.) The Cooper Union office is about two blocks from the Bureau of Engineering and about a mile from the Bureau of Enforcement.

This is the physical reality within which the engineers and inspectors work. Their complaints about their working conditions are vociferous, and presumably their physical circumstances directly affect their functioning and attitude. The Department was not always physically divided and housed in such strikingly disparate environments. Until 1967 the entire Department was housed in a building close to City Hall and the Municipal Building. When the Department expanded in 1966, more space was needed. The commissioner at that time, Austin Heller, felt that housing in or near a university would be beneficial to the Department; his choice was Cooper Union. Unfortunately, there was not space for everybody, so the Department was segmented. Executives and lab staff went to Cooper Union, the engineers to a nearby building, and the inspectors to a building further away. It has since become clear that any benefits derived by top executives directly, or by osmosis, from an intellectual research environment are clearly outweighed by the obvious disadvantage of dividing the top staff of an organization whose primary function is enforcement from the enforcing personnel.26

The Inspectors

How many working inspectors are there? It took four interviews among top management to learn the answer to this question.[27]

In 1971 there were 86 budgeted inspector slots. As of December 1970, two were vacant. (During an interview with Commissioner Rickles, a call came through from Mayor Lindsay's assistant, Sid Davidoff. The vacancies were described as $85 to $96 a week jobs which Davidoff, who was in charge of patronage, might be interested in filling.)

About 5 of the slots are occupied by persons on terminal leave (accumulated overtime, sickness, and vacation time, which civil service personnel may accumulate until retirement—if a man retires on January 1 and has a year's terminal leave, his position cannot be filled until the following January 1.) About 13 of the slots are occupied by persons suspended from their jobs in February 1970 for taking bribes. (This group represented about 15 percent of the budgeted positions, including a high-ranking inspector formerly in charge of court activities. Until they were tried, their slots remain vacant because, should they be found not guilty, the city must pay them the salary they would have earned during the suspension period.) In addition, the Franchise Department, which is not part of the Air Resources Department and has 7 inspectors, will "soon" be authorized to help out by ticketing smoking autos.[28]

Thus, of the 86 budgeted slots there were 66 working inspectors. Most were well-qualified, experienced personnel, but 23 were provisional employes hired without having passed the appropriate civil service test. The major disadvantage of provisional employes is that they are usually inexperienced, and if they fail to pass the test someone else must be hired.

In a 1970 study the federal government estimated that New York City required 182 field inspectors to "adequately" enforce its Air Pollution Control Code.[29] The manpower predictive model from which this number is drawn assumed one inspection per year of each source of stationary emissions, as is done in the west. George Walsh of the federal Environmental Protection Agency, who constructed the model, testified that this number is conservative as applied to New York City and its special problems, such as the necessity of sending inspectors out in pairs in unsafe neighborhoods.[30] Assuming a need for about 200 inspectors, the record to date is dismal. In 1964 there were 36 budgeted slots, in 1968 about 60 budgeted slots, and in 1970 a total of 86 budgeted slots and 66 working inspectors. And, as we shall see, only about half the working inspectors are in the field at any given time. In summary, the Bureau of Enforcement has always been and is now woefully understaffed.

Salary

Inspectors earn $9,000 to $15,000 per annum, but according to Pieratti, "There are few in the upper ranges."[31] A senior inspector earns about $11,000; a supervisory inspector about $12,000; and a single principal inspector, $15,000. Policemen earn more money, while building inspectors earn about the same amount.

Nature of Work

Clerical Desk Jobs. According to Fensterstock, the former director of Program and Planning "The inspection bureau is chronically short of clerical help, and since the formation of the superagency our experienced, well-trained clerks are often transferred to Sanitation." The reason, he said, is that "Sanitation is large, we are small, and there is no place for a first-rate experienced clerk to go here."[32]

On December 11, 1970, the inspectors were short 9 clerks out of their budgeted slots, and on February 24, 1971, they were short 6 clerks out of their budgeted slots. Inspectors must therefore do clerical work to fill the clerical gap, as well as do the clerical work ordinarily required of them. In 1970 inspectors spent 37,586 hours doing office work, 6,504 hours doing court work, 40,706 hours in the field, and 7,543 hours training new inspectors (3,482 hours were classified as miscellaneous).[33]

In addition, inspectors feel that they are required to do a lot of unnecessary paperwork. Pieratti said,

> One of our problems is that they [management] have tried to duplicate other efforts in the country and it just doesn't work here. Our record-keeping was copied from L.A. and we simply don't have the people and money to do the paperwork. . . .
>
> Yes, we have computers. The specialists come in and instead of assisting us, we were required to take men off the job to feed the computer. We've gotten nothing out of it yet. The information is not validated and kept up to date so we haven't gotten a thing out of the computers. We don't even have adequate people to do typing for the courts. . . . In addition daily diaries are required of each inspector, the only purpose of which is to satisfy the Bureau of Investigations. . . . Creates fantastic paperwork. . . . Summaries should be our only required paperwork. What if policemen had to keep such diaries?[34]

In 1971 a comparative study of each inspector's "output" (number of summonses served) was initiated. Inspectors turning in less than an average number of summonses were then called in to explain themselves. The impetus for this procedure was a threat by the city's Bureau of the Budget that in order to survive each department must pay its own way. Summons counting is efficient and simple, whatever the rationale; it is unclear why the diary-keeping continues.)[35]

Field Work. Inspectors operate in three borough teams, each theoretically consisting of 14 persons supervised by a senior inspector. According to Fred Hart, the deputy commissioner responsible for day-to-day enforcement, "There are 27 to 43 inspectors out in the field on any given day, many of them assigned to special duties." One team operates in Manhattan, one in Brooklyn and Staten Island, and one in Queens and the Bronx. "The City is divided into 60 grids," Hart said, "and the team goes in for 2 or 3 days at a time. They operate by putting one or two men on a roof to spot for the two guys in the car."

Hart added, "I try to spend the first hour of each day out in the field. In Heller's time inspection was entirely divorced and alienated from administration." Asked to estimate violations, he said, "There are probably 60,000 violations a day, and we catch only about 600 a month."[36]

Do helicopters help? According to Pieratti,

> Helicopters are a lot of public relations. We have use of one police helicopter. It goes out two or three times a week. We develop the picture and then an inspector follows up with a summons. It takes an inspector one week's work with the follow-up. The point is we still have to send an inspector down to serve the summons. The copter costs $100,000 a year just to house and service. That would pay for ten additional inspectors.[37]

"Specials." Four inspectors supervised by a principal inspector (the highest-paid inspector) are permanently assigned to this work, formerly called "mayor specials." They handle the complaints of VIPs. Some complaints are clearly important, others appear questionable. The job is resentfully carried out by the Bureau of Enforcement. It should be quickly added that "specials" are not a Lindsay invention. According to Pieratti, "They go way back. . . . Specials still occupy a great deal of time. Each person feels that if he is militant and abusive enough he will get corrective action, but it cannot operate that way. We must have a systemized approach, not fragmentized."[38]

During an interview on "specials" with Pieratti and Liebowitz, I observed how they can operate. Harold Glicksman, principal inspector in charge of specials, came into the office to complain that the N.Y.C. Environmental Protection Administration had put through a complaint of smoke in a school that was so bad that children had to be evacuated. Clearly it was an emergency requiring immediate action. Two of Glicksman's inspectors were out sick, one was in the Bronx, and the school was in an unsafe area where inspectors normally operate only in pairs, so Glicksman had to go to the school with one of his men. When he arrived he learned that the complaint was one month old. (Query: Why didn't he telephone first?). Leibowitz told Glicksman not to accept any more phone complaints, "Make them write it down," he said. Pieratti said the incident was not unusual.[39]

Citizen Complaints. Prior to 1966 the Department investigated nearly every complaint, but the records show that investigations originating with citizen complaints generally resulted in few summonses. The enforcement technique thus appeared inefficient as compared to field patrols. The Department now investigates only about a quarter of the citizen complaints it receives (see Tables A.3 and A.4). "We get about 35,000 complaints a year," Pieratti said. "We send an inspector out on about 8,000 of those complaints. We do what we can."[40] (Prior to February 1971 industrial pollution was handled strictly on a complaint and field-spotting basis, so such complaints were more likely to get consideration than boiler or incinerator complaints, which the Department was handling through equipment upgrading provisions.[41])

What about the citizen smoke watchers? This group was first organized by Citizens for Clean Air and trained by the Department. Two contradictory views were presented on their success. On January 8, 1971, Pieratti said, "they served a total of three summonses. Our time is consumed in checking out their stories, and I bet the three summonses get thrown out of court because the inspector never saw the smoke or equipment."[42] In contrast is a letter from the Department's Public Relations Office dated April 30, 1971, and sent to interested citizen groups: "The work of the first group of volunteers, who were trained last fall, has proved very successful, and based on this experience we are looking forward to the establishment of regular training programs in the future."[43]

Informal Hearings. As of January 1971 Field Services again handled informal hearings. Repeat violators, Local Law 14 violators, and engineering violators are called in. Pieratti said, "Deputy Commissioner Hart with Deputy Commissioners Romer and Simon were originally going to be the Departmental hearing officers. Evidently they found it a bigger can of worms than they cared to handle so it's back to Field Services."

In December 1970 Hart said that he personally was handling all these hearings and "we are getting about 100 in a month."[44] There are no records of the hearings, not even a list, other than Hart's personal calendar and a notation on the premises record of the violator. He said he had held 340 hearings himself, but it is impossible to evaluate the effectiveness of such procedures.

Two Typical Workdays

The inspector's working day begins at 8:00 a.m. and ends at 4:00 p.m., five days a week excluding holidays. The two days to be described are January 7 and April 1, 1971.

On January 8, 1971, during an interview on the Bureau of Enforcement's operation, Pieratti asked Leibowitz to give the previous day's breakdown, saying that it was probably typical; the April 1 date was chosen by Leibowitz as a "typical day" for the purpose of demonstrating to the Department's director of Program and Planning. "The severe handicap under which the Bureau of Enforcement operates. . . . The continued lack of manpower for both clerical and inspectorial staff in all classifications."[45]

On January 7, 1971, the inspectors were occupied as follows: 39 in the field, 4 of whom were new and on job training; 4 assigned to court (including paperwork); 1 on radio desk; 3 on special service complaints ("specials"); 2 on asbestos detail; 5 on Local Law 14 office summons writing; 1 assigned to interdepartmental liaison work ("mail bag"); 1 assigned as Department safety officer; and 9 on leave (6 sick leave, 2 annual leave, and 1 emergency leave). The total number of inspectors thus accounted for is 65.[46]

On April 1, 1971, the inspectors were occupied as follows: 10 on Local Law 14 field summons service; 4 on Local Law 14 office summons writing; 6 on field "saturation drive" (teams concentrating on smoke complaints drawn from citizen complaints or a priority list designated by the commissioner or a community group); 6 in the field on compactor inspection*; 2 in the field on "discontinuance inspection" (making sure that incinerators owners claim to have closed down are not being used); 2 in the field on industrial inspection; 1 in the field sealing incinerators; 6 assigned to court (including paperwork); 1 on

---

*When asked why the 6 air pollution control inspectors were checking nonpolluting installations when the Building Department must also inspect the compactors because they are building alterations, Pieratti said, "If you waited for the Building Department to notify us, hell could freeze over. This is high priority for us. There is, you know, a certain lack of communication between departments."

asbestos detail; 2 on the helicopter unit; 5 on special service complaints; 1 on weed detail; 1 assigned to fuel oil sampling for sulfur content; 7 on office paperwork; 1 assigned to serving summonses for the commissioner; 1 assigned to automobile coordinator (coordinating official city cars); 1 on radio desk; and 8 on leave (6 sick leave, 1 annual leave, and 1 jury duty). The total number of inspectors thus accounted for is 64.[47]

Tables A.1 and A.2 in the Statistical Appendix give some indication of inspection activities on an annual basis.

Morale

Observations of Field Services on and off since 1963 lead to the conclusion that during Commissioner Heller's time, morale sunk to an extremely low level. Both Commissioner Rickles and Deputy Commissioner Hart confirmed this conclusion. Rickles said,

> Morale has improved; management has improved. Inspectors are more closely supervised. Aside from dishonesty, many were simply not working. The last administration left me with headaches. They hired lots of provisional people, they gave lots of overtime which I inherit in the form of leaves. . . . Also, in the past they spent a great deal of time answering complaints and sitting around the office.[48]

Hart said the past was "awful":

> It was a research oriented organization and the greatest executive effort went into monitoring. . . . Department's function is enforcement. . . . In Heller's time inspectors were entirely divorced and alienated from administration. There is still great suspicion among them because the informers (everyone knows who they are) were left in the Bureau so everyone feels watched.[49]

Has there been much change in morale? No. Although the present commissioners blame inspector dishonesty and laziness, which admittedly is part of the picture, other factors appear to be contributing more heavily to continuing low morale. In considering these factors it is well to remember the overall pressure created by the Lindsay administration's political commitment to clean up the city's air, since clean air was a major portion of Lindsay's campaigns in 1965 and 1969, when posters read, "Breath Easier, Sleep Better, Feel Safer" and another slogan was "Dirty Air, Dirty Lungs, Dirty

Laundry—He'll do something about Air Pollution."[50] The pressure
is on, but totally inadequate resources and powers have been allocated
to the agency in charge of cleaning up the air. And pressure plus
inadequate resources add up to frustration and low morale.

The specific factors causing low morale appear to be:

1. The physical separation of the bureaus from each other and
from top management, and the disparate conditions of working environments.

2. The lack of a significant promotional ladder. Air Pollution
Control is a small agency with a staff of less than 300; top management
is hired from the outside.

3. The chronic staff shortages and inability to replace staff
because of a city job freeze.

4. The tie-up in courts.

5. The unrealistic nature of the Code. Serious inspectors take
their jobs literally and seriously. "We do what the old Code told us
to do, and here we are expanding on this. We have laws on the books
we can't enforce—we are going from crisis to crisis," Pieratti said.[51]

6. The existence of a superagency. Pieratti said, "Weight within
the organization is determined by numbers. Sanitation has about
20,000 with a hardhitting union, Water Resources 3 or 4,000 and we
have 300. Our commissioner used to report directly to the Mayor,
now he has little control over his own department."[52]

7. The transient nature of top management. "We know these
political appointees wouldn't stay longer, they are in for the short-
term profit [the management turnover record since 1966 is high], and
each time they must be shown that our systems are all right," said
Pieratti.[53]

8. The lack of real power. As Pieratti put it, "We can't shut
down equipment, we can't repair equipment. We can only determine
what an owner should do, and if he doesn't, we go through the minimal
fine revolving door. I suggested the use of portable steam boilers,
so we could shut down smoking boilers in the winter, but the higher-
ups nixed it."[54]

9. The nature of the violators. Pieratti said, "We know who
they are. They are not home owners with pride like in L. A. They
are tough. Financial survival depends on least cost manipulations
. . . they would grab any loophole or opportunity."[55]

Some Solutions Proposed by Inspectors

"The long-term goal must be to eliminate sources," said
Schechter. "It takes courage to do this. This is where Heller got
into trouble the first time. He said, 'we must eventually eliminate
private incineration' and they said, 'How can you say this when you

30

are trying to get the landlords to fork up $7-9,000?' What little participation in policymaking allowed us has always been against private incineration."56

Asked about administrative hearings, including the power to fine, and about tagging equipment (like traffic tickets) instead of having to personally serve the owner, Pieratti and Liebowitz agreed enthusiastically. "The criminal courts thing is a big waste of time and money. We'll never get anywhere," Pieratti said.

Pieratti suggests it would be a good idea "to hook up portable heaters to illegal boilers, seal the boiler and charge the owner the rental [$600 a day]. This way tenants don't suffer and we have the stick we need."

Liebowitz said, "We must get the trucks out of the city between 8 a.m. and 5 p.m. The traffic thing is impossible because of air pollution and noise. Set up depots around the city and transfer goods to smaller trucks and make the unions work at night."57

Although these proposals are incomplete, and the pros and cons more complex than stated, they do show that the operating people have ideas that are well-grounded in physical if not in political reality.

The Engineers

There are 18 budgeted engineer slots. Six slots were vacant as of early 1971, leaving a grand total of 12 engineers to review the plans and specifications of about 75,000 pieces of equipment, to issue work permits, to make physical inspections when work is completed, and to issue certificates of operation if the equipment conforms to the plans and specifications. They do not check the equipment's performance. A fee of about $50 to $100 is charged, which is supposed to equal the cost to the city of processing the paperwork.58

The foregoing duties are absurd enough given only 12 engineers, but in addition Commissioner Rickles told the New York City Council Committee on Environmental Protection:

Virtually every plan that comes into the Department is incorrect. The contractors, and they employ engineers, make money by cutting corners. If you gave me a penny for every dishonest plan filed, I could retire a millionaire.

Asked if he meant engineers were filing improper plans, Rickles said:

I'll bring you 160 from my basket right now. I was more willing to believe people 14 months ago. Even the Board of Education tried to get away with putting in old pieces of equipment. . . . If correct plans were filed it would take us about 5 to 6 weeks to issue a work permit. Nearly all the plans are not, so we issue objections and that takes a couple weeks. We need additional manpower. We need clerks. Our problem is backlog. With proper manpower we could do the job.[59]

In addition to the large-scale filing of improper plans, money and time is consumed in needless inspections. Pieratti said:

Many owners use our engineers to do their private contracting work. They say the work is done. The inspector goes out and the equipment is not operating. Problems have developed, and the inspector is called in instead of the contractor. It's much cheaper that way.

Pieratti added that for one week he charged $30 for each application for an operating certificate (rather than a flat fee for the certificate). Applications were cut down considerably and he obtained 75 percent approvals instead of the usual 35 percent. But owners put the pressure on Kretchmer and Commissioner Rickles, and the system was dropped. "Everyone is trying to get someone else to do the work they are being paid for," Pieratti said.[60]

ENFORCEMENT STRATEGY

Agency enforcement strategy is dictated by necessity—the bare minimum for keeping up with the problem—and by the licensing requirements dictated by Local Law 14. There is not now, nor was there ever, a rational overall Department plan for controlling air pollution in New York City. As situations arise the Department reacts as best as it can. An illustration is the policy on repeat offenders. "We don't keep a general record of repeat offenders, Pieratti said. "We don't need it because we have a wealth of information as to who to hit. We get it from the Commissioner, mayor 'specials,' things like that. We have more than we can handle. We are not searching for new customers."[61]

Prior to 1965 the Department was very small and very unimportant. Its resources were ludicrously inadequate in terms of the job to be done. Long-term strategy was impossible, so the Department adopted two tactics: It responded very heavily to citizen complaints (a little patrol work also was done) and kept track of repeat offenders, calling them in for informal hearings, and from time to time threatening to seal polluting equipment, although it never was sealed.[62]

The passage of Local Law 14 in 1966 forced upon the Department the job of requiring every owner (private and public) of a boiler or incinerator in the city to upgrade his equipment. There are at least 75,000 boilers and incinerators, nearly all owned by governmental agencies (state and city) or by businesses that own and operate multiple dwellings, which openly opposed the across-the-board upgrading of all equipment on grounds that it was too expensive (the cost is about $5,000 to $8,000). By 1967 it was clear that noncompliance with Local Law 14's first deadline was almost universal. Since that time, most (and at times all) of the Department's enforcement resources have been devoted to trying to carry out the upgrading mandates of Local Law 14. For limited periods of time, when a big upgrading push is on, general enforcement may come to a virtual standstill because the staff is not sufficient to do both at once.

Another major tactic of Local Law 14 was to regulate the kind of fuel consumed. The Department successfully carried out the mandate with respect to the sulfur content of fuel, but failed to enforce the ban on soft coal. The soft coal users sued, and the case was settled: The city permitted the burning of the outlawed coal provided that the grade satisfied the sulfur content standards of the law, despite the additional problems of particulate matter and other pollutants produced by soft coal (see Chapter 4).

From 1966 through 1969, under Commissioner Heller, the Department's focus appeared to be the establishment of the city's many monitoring stations. The effort was to put the Department on a scientific, statistical, computerized basis. Legal strategy did not fit into the scheme of things, and enforcement was not a principal focus.[63]

After Lindsay's reelection as mayor in 1969, a new commissioner was appointed, Robert Rickles, who publicly stated "The primary job of the agency is enforcement."[64] However, whatever his personal belief, the commissioner was still limited by other factors:

1. Pollution sources are too numerous and unprofessionally operated ever to be effectively policed, so these sources will continue to sap Department resources regardless of the quantity or quality of such resources.

2. Department attorneys are prohibited from representing the Department in court, thus making it virtually impossible for them to carry out the Department's legal strategies.

3. The Bureau of the Budget has requested the Department "to make a profit"—to engage in activities that will maximize the amount of revenue collected. This policy clearly does nothing to advance air pollution control planning.[65]

33

The Department's enforcement efforts over the past 20 years have been almost exclusively devoted to controlling pollution from household boilers and incinerators, and from Con Edison power plants. Other major sources have been almost entirely ignored or have received fitful and frustrating attention: for industrial emissions, a systematic control program began in February 1971; motor vehicles of all sorts are largely covered by sporadic drives, although city bus engines are better maintained (in the past they spewed visible fumes); scattered street closings may create more air pollution on other streets; bridge tolls designed to limit the number of cars entering Manhattan were turned down by the Port Authority, borough presidents, and N.Y. State Legislature; a proposed midtown parking tax never got out of legislative committee in Albany; pollution from commercial sources such as dry cleaners, gasoline stations, and garages is ignored; attempts to regulate construction and demolition (except for asbestos spraying) apparently were squelched by the building trades, Building Department, and the City Council.

SELECTION OF POLLUTORS FOR COURT ACTION

How does the Department select violators for court action? Traditionally, court action against a violator begins when an inspector actually sees a violation. A summons may or may not be issued on the spot, depending on the nature of the violation. The unwritten policy is to immediately serve a summons on the operator of equipment for a "smoke" violation. The Department treats the operator, not the owner, as responsible for the equipment's operation—a questionable assumption. In almost all instances, these summonses involve emissions from boilers or incinerators.[66]

Equipment violations (other than Local Law 14 upgrading violations) and failure of a superintendent or operator to have a Local Law 14 operating certificate initally are treated informally. The inspector serves a violation notice (warning) on the operator of the equipment and requests that the condition be corrected before he returns to reinspect. If there is still an equipment violation after reinspection, the inspector tries to serve a summons on the owner, not the operator, because the Department considers the owner responsible for the equipment's maintenance and repair. The Department has a tremendous backlog of violation notices, 12,000 at the end of 1970.[67] The procedure is thus inefficient and difficult to rationalize. Why should equipment deficiencies be treated as lesser violations than smoke emissions and require a double inspection? Cynically, one might view this as a convenient method of obtaining bribes, since it gives the owner ample warning of an impending summons. A more practical reason for this procedure is that it is difficult and expensive to serve a summons on a building owner. The hope is that the notice will cause compliance without legal coercion.

In 1971 the Department departed from its tradition of serving a summons only after actually seeing a violation, and from its tradition of serving a notice rather than a summons on equipment violations. The Department began serving summonses for failure to apply for a permit to upgrade a boiler or incinerator as required by Local Law 14, instead of for failure to install the upgraded equipment. The complaint is on the basis of Department records rather than an inspection; if there is a mistake because of incorrect records, the summonses are immediately withdrawn.[68]

The second departure from tradition is the use of "orders to show cause why the equipment should not be sealed." In winter 1971, for the first time in the Department's 20-year history, about 70 such orders were served on Local Law 14 upgrading violators with particularly bad records, and about 10 were sealed.[69]

The Department also initiated a policy of serving orders to show cause on industrial equipment violations beginning with the worst ones in terms of the quantity and quality of emissions. Most of these industrial violators do not have any air pollution control permits—not for their industrial equipment, not for their boilers, and not for their incinerators. Will they be sealed? Undoubtedly not, based on the past pattern. The Department is requiring industry to appear at an informal hearing. Its hope is that industry will understand the need for compliance and voluntarily agree to comply within an agreed period of time. This policy also has not been notably successful in the past.[70]

As a result of these procedures, what types of violations end up in court—or, in other words, what type of violations does the Department select for court action? Summons statistics go back to 1968 and show three classifications: smoke (boilers and incinerators), motor vehicle emissions, and Local Law 14 and others (including licensing and general equipment or control apparatus violations). These classifications were changed in 1970 to defective equipment, Local Law 14—incinerator, and Local Law 14—residual. The record shows the following summonses served:

	Boiler smoke	Incinerator smoke	Motor vehicle	Local Law 14 and others	Total summonses
1968	1,344	292	352	690	2,678
1969	1,243	221	69	2,989	4,522

	Defective equipment	Local Law 14—incinerator	Local Law 14—residual oil	Total
1970	3,563	534	206	4,303

Clearly generalizations cannot be made from such limited and varied statistics.[71]

There are also statistics available on the kinds of sources that receive summonses:[72]

	Multiple dwelling	Commercial	Motor vehicle	Power plant	Miscellaneous (including industrial)
1968	1,863	310	346	12	147
1969	3,994	179	69	52	228

NOTES

1. N.Y.C. Charter and Administrative Code, ch. 26, Title D. The Department was granted licensing powers while it was still a bureau within the Department of Housing and Buildings: N.Y.C. Adm. Code, ch. 57, sec. 1403.2-5.01 (1971).
2. Rules and Regulations including fee schedule for the issuance of Permits and Certificates in Conformance with Chapter 47 of the Administrative Code of the City of N.Y., effective May 15, 1954, Rule 2.
3. Dialogue between Commissioner Robert Rickles and Councilman Katz during Executive Session of the New York City Council, Committee on Environmental Protection, May 7, 1971.
4. Interviews with Pieratti, January 8, 1971, and Radzka, April 21, 1971.
5. N.Y.C. Air Pollution Code, Art. 5 (1964), amended N.Y.C. Adm. Code, Apr. 5 (1971).
6. Interviews with Rickles, December 11, 1970, and Pieratti, April 12, 1971.
7. Pieratti, April 12, 1971.
8. Supra notes 53, 54, 55 of Chapter 1
9. Rickles, May 7, 1971.
10. N.Y.C. Adm. Code, 41, sec. 982-6.0 (1951).
11. N.Y.C. Air Pollution Control Code, sec. 3.09 (1964).
12. N.Y.C. Adm. Code, ch. 41, sec. 892-6.0 (1966); N.Y.C. Adm. Code. ch. 57, sec. 1403.2-15.01 (b) (3) (1971). Since 1971 power to seal has been transferred from the Department to the N.Y.C. Environmental Control Board.
13. New York Daily News, February 1971.
14. Interviews with Rickles and Kramer, spring 1971.
15. Interview with Kramer, April 9, 1971.
16. N.Y.C. Adm. Code, ch. 57 sec. 1403.2-3.01 (1971) (general powers).

17. N.Y. Law Journal, Nov. 18, 1971, at 19, La Monica v. Kretchmer, Riccobono, J. (N.Y. City Sup. Co.)

18. N.Y.C. Air Pollution Control Code, sec. 3.07 (1964) amended ch. 57, sec. 1403.2-15.01 (b) (2) (d) (1971).

19. N.Y.C. Adm. Code, ch. 57, sec. 1403.2-3.05 (1971).

20. Testimony of Commissioner Rickles, Executive Session, N.Y. City Council, Committee on Environmental Protection, May 1971.

21. Interview with Romer, January 15, 1971.

22. Interviews with Rickles, Hart, Pieratti, and Schechter, spring 1971.

23. Interviews with Hart, Pieratti, and Schechter, spring 1971.

24. Interdepartmental memo from Joseph Schechter entitled "Methods of Controlling Inspectors," undated.

25. Interview with Pieratti, January 8, 1971.

26. Interview with Dorfman and interviews with Kowald, February 16, 1971.

27. Interviews with Rickles, December 11, 1971; Hart, December 12, 1971; Fensterstock, December 11, 1971; Pieratti and Leibowitz, January 8, 1971.

28. December 11, 1971.

29. Manpower and Training Needs for Air Pollution Control, report of the section of the Department of Health, Education and Welfare, to Congress in compliance with Public Law 90-148, Clean Air Act as amended (June 1970), prepared by George Walsh.

30. Testimony of George Walsh, public hearings on the proposed revision of the New York City air pollution control law, January 27, 1971. The figure of 182 was given by Walsh in response to a question by Councilman Weiss: "If the federal estimate is that a minimum total staff of 500 is needed for New York City (we now have 260), what percentage should be doing field inspection work?" Walsh replied, "the figures were conservative with respect to New York City because they are based on a national manpower predictive model which does not take into consideration such New York City problems as how fast can an inspector travel, necessity of going in pairs to unsafe areas, length of time an inspection takes, length of time it takes to serve an owner with a summons, etc." (See report for fact that states have overstaffed themselves and understaffed localities); Department annual reports, 1964 and 1968. Interview Pieratti, 1/8/71.

31. Interview with Fensterstock, December 11, 1970.

32. Ibid.

33. Ibid.

34. Interview with Pieratti, January 8, 1971.

35. Interview with Leibowitz, January 8, 1971; interview with Fensterstock, December 21, 1970.

36. Interview with Hart, December 21, 1970.

37. Interview with Pieratti, April 12, 1971.
38. Interview with Pieratti and Leibowitz, January 8, 1971.
39. Ibid.
40. Ibid. An intradepartmental memo entitled "Monthly Reconciliation of Inspector's Activities—Yearly Total for 1970," dated March 11, 1971, shows a total of 8,140 citizen complaint inspections for 1970; an intradepartmental memo entitled "Comparison of Yearly Totals (1956-1966) Inspector's Activities" shows that the number of citizen complaint inspections was cut in half in 1966 to the present figure of about 8,000. This is interesting, since prior to 1966 there were half as many inspectors. The figures show the following:

Year	Citizen complaint inspections
1957	15,168
1958	11,377
1959	12,925
1960	11,116
1961	14,026
1962	14,412
1963	14,434
1964	16,304
1965	18,960
1966	8,637

Note: Annual complaints of 40,000 is the commonly quoted figure, but Department statistics on citizen complaints show the number received in recent years to be 5,-10,000 fewer. See Table A.3 in Statistical Appendix.
41. Pieratti and Leibowitz, January 8, 1971.
42. Interview with Pieratti, January 2, 1971.
43. Letter dated April 30, 1971 from Barbara Simpson, Public Information Officer, sent to interested citizen groups and addressed "Dear Citizen."
44. Interviews with Pieratti and Leibowitz, January 8, 1971; interview with Hart, December 21, 1970.
45. Interviews at Bureau of Enforcement on January 8 and April 12, 1971; Intradepartmental memo to Fensterstock from Leibowitz entitled "Bureau Operations," dated April 1, 1971.
46. Intradepartmental form, untitled, dated January 8, 1971.
47. Intradepartmental memo to Fensterstock from Leibowitz, dated April 1, 1971, entitled "Bureau Operations"; interview with Pieratti, April 21, 1971.
48. Interview with Rickles, December 11, 1971.

49. Interview with Hart, December 21, 1970.
50. Slogan is from a speech by former Commissioner Heller before the Traveler's Research Center, March 28, 1968.
51. Interview with Pieratti, January 2, 1971.
52. Ibid.
53. Ibid.
54. Ibid.
55. Ibid.
56. Interview with Schechter, January 8, 1971.
57. Interview with Pieratti and Leibowitz, January 8, 1971.
58. Interviews with Rickles, December 11, 1971; Hart, December 12, 1971; Fensterstock, December 11, 1971; Pieratti and Liebowitz, January 8, 1971.
59. Testimony of Rickles, Executive Session of the New York City Council, Committee on Environmental Protection, spring 1971.
60. Interview with Pieratti, April 12, 1971.
61. Interview with Pieratti, April 12, 1971. Federal Clean Air Act of 1970, sec. 110, now requires the development and implementation of a plan to achieve federal air quality standards by 1975.
62. Department annual reports, 1960-65; interviews with Benline, Wolff, and Glicksman, 1963 and 1964; interview with Pieratti, April 12, 1971.
63. Interview with Heller, December 4, 1968.
64. Interview with Rickles, December 11, 1970.
65. Interview with Hart, December 21, 1970, and Fensterstock December 21, 1970.
66. Interviews with Pieratti and Leibowitz, January 8, 1971. Examination of court docket sheets shows the operator as defendant in the case of a smoke violation and the owner or agent in case of an equipment violation.
67. Untitled Intradepartmental report dated March 1971, states that the inspection backlog at the close of 1970 numbered 12,000.
68. Interviews with Pieratti, January 8, 1971, and Kramer, April 9, 1971.
69. Interview with Kramer, April 9, 1971; testimony of Rickles at Executive Session of the New York City Council, Committee on Environmental Protection, spring 1971.
70. Interview with Radzka, spring 1971.
71. Intradepartmental memo entitled "Summonses Served Type of Violation and Source," undated.
72. Ibid.

CHAPTER

3

GETTING THE POLLUTOR
TO COURT

In order to get an alleged pollutor to court he must be personally served with a summons.[1] Why personal service? Why not mail the summons to the pollutor, or attach it to the offending equipment, as the police do with traffic tickets?

For violation of the N.Y.C. Air Pollution Control Code there are criminal penalties that can only be enforced by a criminal court. A criminal court does not have jurisdiction and cannot decide a case, even a "noncriminal" Code offense or violation, without personal service and the appearance of the alleged violator. Criminal procedure is understandable if one thinks in terms of traditional crime: Constitutional guarantees of due process demand that the accused be personally informed of the nature of the accusation and present in the court for the hearing on his crime. But criminal procedures are ludicrous in the case of Code violations that should carry civil penalties, such as littering, double-parking, failure to curb a dog, and numerous other offenses committed daily in the metropolitan area. (Civil penalties were added to criminal penalties in 1971).

Once the defendant is properly served, the court still does not have jurisdiction in the case of an individual. A criminal court is powerless to proceed with a case until the individual defendant physically appears in court. If the defendant fails to appear, the court can exercise its power to issue a warrant for arrest. The Air Resources Department requests the court to issue a warrant on the nonappearing defendant, and the court warrant officer attempts to find the defendant by checking a variety of sources for an address. The officer then mails a notice calling on the defendant to appear in court on a specified day or be subject to arrest. Meanwhile the summons is kept by the warrant officer. If the defendant is caught and brought before the court, the defendant may be fined for contempt of court for failure to obey the summons.[2]

In the case of personal service on a corporation, which is accomplished by serving an officer or agent, the court does obtain full jurisdiction. It is impossible to arrest a corporation and bring it physically before the court; when a corporation fails to appear the court may punish it for contempt. But in practice, this is not done. Instead of a warrant, the court mails an inquest requesting the corporation's appearance.[3]

The Department calls warrants "sewer service."[4] Department members are bitter because a fairly large number of defendants do not show up in court and the warrant procedure does not bring them in. In July 1969 there was a backlog of 1,000 outstanding warrants. In June 1970 there were 1,599 outstanding warrants out of a total of 2,329 outstanding cases (outstanding cases are cases adjourned, or cases where warrants and inquests have been issued). By the end of 1970 there were 9,310 outstanding cases (adjournments, warrants, and inquests) out of a total of 12,699 cases brought to court. (Of the 3,309 resolved cases, 325 were dismissed, 282 withdrawn, and 2,702 convicted at an average fine of $35.)[5]

Personal service of a summons on the owner of the equipment is a time-consuming task. According to Alfred Pieratti, the executive director of Engineering and Enforcement, "When a drive is on we are told to 'Serve summonses like confetti'. It takes a half-day's work to serve one Local Law 14 summons if the files are in good shape and ready to move. So how many owners can we hit in one day? They tell us to serve 'em like confetti. Even if we put all the men on summons serving, we can serve maybe 20 to 25 a day."[6]

An inspector normally can serve an average of 1.7 individual summonses a day, unless more than one summons is served on the same owner at the same time, as can be done on per diem violations. Most defendants are landlords and some, particularly the hard-core, repeat violators, are not easy to find. They hide behind the veil of multiple corporations and other legal devices. This is a familiar and unsolved problem for other city agencies as well.[7]

To avoid personal service the Department tries from time to time to use informal procedures in the hope of obtaining compliance without timeconsuming legalities. It uses violation notices, or insofar as possible serves the operator-employee rather than the absent, responsible owner-employer. The Department also has used service by mail, which is legally ineffective if the defendant fails to appear since the court does not have jurisdiction and cannot proceed with the case. If the defendant voluntarily appears he is actually conferring jurisdiction on the court, and "well-advised" violators do not volunteer. Although other city agencies routinely start by mailing summonses and are reputed to obtain a high voluntary response, the Department does not. It found that the response to mailed violation notices was so poor it was not worth the double workload.[8] For example, in 1969 about 23,000 violation notices were mailed for failure to upgrade boilers and incinerators as required by Local Law 14; the response was virtually zero (see Chapter 2).

CRIMINAL COURT PROCEDURES AND
SENTENCING PRACTICES

Unfortunately, for nearly 20 years the enforcement of New York City's air pollution control laws depended solely on criminal prosecution. Until 1971, in order to curb a violator, the city's only remedy was to prosecute the violator in a criminal court that could impose a fine or imprison the defendant.

Since 1971 alternative civil penalties may be imposed by a newly created Environmental Control Board.[9] However, the board was appointed only recently, early in 1973, and therefore the effectiveness of alternative administrative procedures and civil penalties cannot be evaluated.

Air pollution control violations are prosecuted in Part 6 of the New York City Criminal Court in the counties of New York, the Bronx, Kings, and Queens. (In Staten Island there are so few municipal cases that there is no special part.) Criminal Court is divided into 10 parts, and Part 6 is known as the municipal term. All violations brought by any city agency other than the police department are prosecuted in Part 6.[10] Air pollution cases are routinely heard on a different day of the week in each of the counties containing a Part 6. Four different assistant corporation counsels plead the air pollution cases, each in the county to which he is "permanently" assigned by the Penalties Division of the Law Department. Thus, for example, each Wednesday the same assistant corporation counsel pleads air pollution control cases in Manhattan.

A senior air pollution control inspector, with a few assistants, is permanently assigned to court duty. He travels from borough to borough during the week, keeps the dockets, and is the only person with a grasp of what is occurring in all the city courts with respect to air pollution cases. Corporation counsel maintains no files with the exception of one on Con Edison. The records, which are maintained in the Department's field service bureau, give the name of the pollutor, address, type of violation, number of previous offenses, pleading, and sentence. The records are filed according to the address of the premises, not the owner's name, so that repeat violations refer to only one premise, not several premises of the same owner. A court stenographer records the proceedings of each court session, but proceedings are not transcribed unless requested and paid for by a party to the action (the cost is high, about $300 a session). Evidence submitted to court is kept there with the minutes, and no transcribed record is kept by corporation counsel or the Department.[11]

Thus, court activities are the responsibility of a few senior inspectors who have relatively low status in the Department hierarchy. Until 1970 no one of any consequence from the Department, attorney or otherwise, had ever been to court. That situation appears to have changed. The City EPA attorneys, the deputy commissioner and the commissioner appear to be aware of the mess that characterizes the city's routine air pollution control prosecutions. If the officials were not totally aware, an article by Steve Lawrence that appeared in the New York Post in spring 1971 surely did the trick. I quote extensively from the article because it is an accurate description of a routine court day. I saw over a dozen similar days myself. Lawrence reports:

> Manhattan Criminal Court, Part Six, doesn't exactly seem to strike fear into the hearts of landlords who pollute the city air with their malfunctioning incinerators and furnaces.
>
> A nuisance; a slight slap on the wrist; endless waiting in a dingy courtroom; . . . a procedure reminiscent of an absurdist drama, it is all of that.
>
> But the owners of the buildings don't even venture into the cavernous corridors of Criminal Court. They send a lawyer, or an agent, or often a building superintendent, who may speak little English, and if he does, he still can't follow or understand the blur of activity as cases are adjourned, landlords fined and complaints dismissed.
>
> "The whole thing is confusion," says one air pollution inspector whose main job is keeping track of cases as they drag through the court process. "Things move so fast, sometimes I get lost."
>
> Yesterday it was Judge Walter Bayer, moving them through. In a half hour he disposed of about 25 cases.
>
> "You mean you have no lawyer and the owner isn't here?" Judge Bayer asked Ludmil Petrov, the bewildered superintendent of a building at 7 Park Avenue. Petrov was insisting he wasn't guilty of anything. The pollution summons, for a smoky oil burner, didn't mean a thing to him.
>
> "Look, you get a lawyer and bring the owner down here," Bayer admonished him. "You can get a criminal record if you're found guilty of this."*

---

*Note that Judge Bayer was imprecise when he told the superintendent of 7 Park Avenue that he could get a "criminal record" if found

Bayer dished out fines in 18 of the 49 cases he heard. The penalties might make a superintendent wince, but were hardly calculated to hurt a building owner. All were $25, the exact minimum required by law. The judge could have handed out $200 fines or 60 days in jail for each offense.

The judge apparently was unimpressed with multiple violations. Jerry Kopito, the agent for a building at 327 Central Park W., had received six summonses. He was fined $25 on two and nothing on the remaining four. The City assistant corporation counsel objected. Bayer called the next case.

With Mort Denker, agent for a building at 101 Cooper St., it was the same story. He had received four summonses, was fined $25 on one and nothing on the other three. Denker previously had been in Part Six and fined $25 once before, in October 1969.

Criminal Court, Part Six, appeared to have cornered the market on rubber stamps. Bam, bam, bam, next case. . . .

It was an average day for pollution complaints, one inspector said. The judge handled 49 complaints on 27 different buildings. Thirteen were in court for the first time. Thirty-six had been there before.

There were eighteen fines, 15 guilty but no fines, 12 not guilty with trial dates set, one arrest warrant issued because the landlord didn't appear, one complaint withdrawn because the Air Resources Dept. had already issued a compliance certificate. And there was one so-called "all-purpose adjournment" because the building in question was to be torn down.[12]

What happens in court? Well, as Lawrence reports, it moves quickly. The procedure is called arraignment. If the defendant appears on the return date specified in the summons, he is "arraigned" in more or less the same manner as a criminal would be in other parts of the court. First a clerk calls the calendar, a kind of roll-call to see who is there. The cases are then heard by the judge in the order in which they appear on the calendar. If a defendant is near the bottom of the list, he may have to wait several hours even though all he wants to do is plead guilty, pay the fine, and get out.

---

guilty. An air pollution violation is an offense, not a misdemeanor. One of the purposes of the "offense" classification, sometimes called a noncrime, is to avoid giving a criminal record to violators.

Unless one operates under the theory that sitting around a courtroom effectively deters polluters (which might work if the owner was there, but usually it is the superintendent or an agent) the system is wasteful and can only result in cynical disregard for the law.

A clerk reads the defendant's name and docket number of his case, and he is told to come forward to the bench to face the judge. The clerk reads the charges and asks if the defendant understands them. If the defendant is non-English-speaking (the courtroom routinely is filled with building superintendents who do not speak English), an attempt is made to find someone in the courtroom to serve as a translator—on one day I spent in court, I was overheard speaking Spanish and asked to help out with Spanish translations.

If the defendant says he understands the charges, he is asked to enter a plea of "guilty," "not guilty," or "guilty with an explanation." The plea of "guilty with an explanation," which is not provided for in the laws of criminal procedures, is recognized and has been used for many years in the lower criminal courts of New York. It is a plea of guilty that allows an opportunity to explain extenuating circumstances to the judge in the hope of getting a minimum fine. It is a very frequently used plea, and almost always works. If the plea is "guilty" or "guilty with an explanation," the court pronounces sentence immediately, that is, announces the amount of the fine. The fine is paid immediately to a clerk, and that ends the proceedings.

With a few exceptions, almost all cases are thus disposed of. Normally, defendants do not plead "not guilty" because the penalty is so small that it is far cheaper and less time-consuming to plead "guilty with an explanation." However, if a large number of defendants made a concerted effort to plead "not guilty," the resulting logjam of cases to be tried would quickly put the calendar months or even years behind schedule. It also would tie up the inspectors because the inspector who saw the violation must be present at the trial. The prosecution of cases could thus be effectively sabotaged.[13]

It appears that a concerted logjam tactic may in fact be coming into use. In late winter 1971 the number of "not guilty" pleas rose sharply from a few hundred to thousands, as the Department attempted for the umpteenth time to enforce the upgrading requirements of Local Law 14. Most cases were adjourned for six months or more to allow the defendant or his counsel time to prepare for trial. But the New York City corporation counsel does not prepare ahead for trials of this sort and does them on the spot with no briefs; when confronted with well-prepared defendants like Con Edison, the city usually loses. Subsequent adjournments are routinely granted (particularly if the defendant is represented by an attorney) for illness, unavailability of all the persons needed for the trial on the same day (the inspector must be present), unavailability of a judge to sit, need of time to prepare the case, and so forth. In addition, since judges are rotated, adjournments are commonly requested in order to avoid a "tough" judge in the hope that an "easier" judge will be sitting on the adjourned date. Under normal conditions a trial may be postponed for at least six months or more by the clever use of adjournments. Thus "not guilty" pleas are very useful if the purpose is to postpone compliance with the law.

If a case is tried, it is before a single judge without a jury. The violation of an air pollution control law belongs to the category of criminal infractions called "offenses" or "violations" which need not be tried before a jury or a bench composed of more than one judge, as is required in regular criminal prosecutions.

The city must prove the defendant's guilt beyond a reasonable doubt. It is one of the anomalies of the law that the offense is treated as noncriminal for the purpose of establishing a criminal record but retains criminal procedures designed for maximum protection of a defendant because of the seriousness of a criminal stigma. Proof beyond a reasonable doubt is a very heavy burden for the defendant wins if he creates any doubt at all in the judge's mind as to the validity of the city's case. This is not difficult to do, for cases are tried by an assistant corporation counsel, without advance preparation other than a brief talk before the trial with the inspector. In addition, the inspector does not know when the trial will occur until an hour or so ahead of time. Since trials are almost always routinely adjourned at the request of the defendant, the inspector is not required to be in court until it is certain there will be a trial. He is telephoned that day and appears just before the trial. Since there is always a large gap from the time of the violation to the time of trial, the result is often a poorly prepared inspector whose memory, understandably, may be faulty. I watched as the city lost one trial because the inspector could not remember a factual detail concerning the direction from which he saw the smoke, although directly after the trial while still in the courtroom he remembered the needed fact.*

Cases also may be disposed of in other ways. Sometimes cases are withdrawn by the assistant corporation counsel if he does not

---

*This trial took place in Manhattan on December 11, 1968. The inspector was not informed ahead of the trial date, and consequently his notes were at home (rather detailed notes are made by the inspectors when they serve a summons in order to aid their recollection of details, should a trial occur). Without notes the inspector could not remember where he was when he observed the smoke. The alleged violator thus managed to create a doubt as to his guilt and win the case. A few minutes after the trial the inspector suddenly remembered exactly where he had stood when he saw the smoke.

think he has enough evidence. A case may be dismissed by a judge if he does not think the charges are sustained by the evidence. A judge also may suspend a sentence if that is recommended by the assistant corporation counsel or if the judge feels the defendant was only technically responsible.[14]

From 1956 to 1973 the Department obtained a 95 percent conviction rate of the total of cases listed as "disposed of," that is, those involving convictions, dismissals, withdrawals, and suspended sentences. However in 1970 the conviction rate dramatically dropped to 82 percent. (The statistics for 1970 were 2,702 convictions, 325 dismissals, and 282 withdrawals.) More important than the lower conviction rate on disposed cases, most air pollution control cases pending before the court were routinely adjourned or required a warrant or inquest. In 1970 only 25 percent of the cases presented were resolved while 75 percent were adjourned. The vast majority of these were Local Law 14 cases, but 30 to 40 percent included regular code violations (see Table A.7 in Statistical Appendix).

Before discussing sentencing practices and the general effectiveness of criminal prosecution, the problems most apparent to an observer of the court scene may be summarized as follows:

1. Most summonses are served on superintendents, agents, or managers, not owners. The owner's name therefore does not generally appear on the record, nor is the owner, or his attorney, in court. The records show the address of the premises and the name of the defendant; if the owner has never been served, his name never appears.

2. The proceedings before the court are not an adversary proceeding between well-prepared counsel. The preparation and presentation of cases is treated as little more than a routine clerical job. The assistant corporation counsel has no knowledge of or stake in the Department's policies, nor does he know the history or seriousness of particular cases except as the docket sheet shows prior convictions of the same defendant. Each case is presented as a separate entity, when in fact many are part of a greater mosaic, as in the case of corporations with more than one plant, or landlords with more than one building. A judge could hardly be expected to appreciate the seriousness of these cases. Consequently cases are routinely treated as trivial.

3. New York City criminal courts are notorious for their wretched facilities and heavy caseloads. At times they also appear to be chronically short of judges. During two winters when I observed the court procedure, some judges naturally failed to appear because of illness. In such instances, all air pollution control cases were postponed because no extra judges were available to substitute. Trials were frequently postponed by the court, or the hearings began an hour or two later than scheduled, and anywhere from 40 to 75 defendants had to sit around waiting for the judge.

4. Rotation of judges is the practice in criminal court. There is therefore no continuity, no expertise, and sometimes, unfortunately, no interest. With the exception of one or two judges, there was often indifference about the case and such issues as who the responsible party really was; and the proceedings often sounded more like an auction than a judicial convocation.

Sentencing practices of the criminal courts destroy whatever deterrent effect the air pollution control law might have. The courts uniformly impose small fines regardless of the seriousness of the violation, and they ignore the number of offenses on record for the premises. It is much, much cheaper to pay a fine than to repair, properly maintain, and operate equipment that pollutes the air. Judging from sentencing records over almost ten years, it is seriously open to question whether the city is needlessly wasting taxpayer money in an expensive charade.

The amount of the fine imposed by the court for an air pollution violation has not changed substantially in the last twenty years: The average fine is still $35. In fact, fines may not have changed much since 1895, when a Brooklyn ordinance set a maximum fine of $100. The average fine remains the same despite the fact that in 1966 the law was amended to raise minimum penalties for a second offense from $50 to $75 (the maximum remained $500) and to create a third offense category with fines of $200 to $1,000 (the fine for a first offense remained $25 to $100).[15] All these penalties carry an alternative of imprisonment, but it is never used.

During a dozen court visits involving 300 or 400 cases, I never heard anything but a minimum fine imposed, and never a fine for a third offense. It would therefore appear that under the present system the only way to increase the fines substantially is to boost the amount of the minimum fine, particularly in the first and second offense categories. The maximum fine operates more as a public relations gimmick—"See how tough we can be with pollutors.' "—than a realistic deterrent.[16]

In addition, fines rarely exceed $200 regardless of the number of offenses at particular premises or plants. The courts treat a violation as a first offense if the named defendant is new, and a high turnover or rotation of employees at a plant insures a ready supply of new defendants. Also, an agent or corporation may be named as a defendant, and each is then treated as a new defendant. If an owner is not clever enough to rotate his employees, the court generally allows substitutions (corporation for the employee or vice versa), or in some cases simply "interprets" the law to allow for a minimum fine, as the Phelps Dodge case shows (see below).[17]

The following are only a few examples of the above practices. The Department's daily docket sheets are filled with thousands of similar cases.

48

The Phelps Dodge Case

In Queens, on November 19, 1970, Donald A Ingvoldstad, an employee of Phelps Dodge Refining Corporation, pleaded guilty to two violations and received a sentence of $50—$25 per count. The record then read:

Name of defendant	Date of disposition	Amount of fine
1. Phelps Dodge Refining Corp.	6/23/66	$150
2. Phelps Dodge Refining Corp.	1/19/67	$250
3. Phelps Dodge Refining Corp.	4/18/68	$350
4. Phelps Dodge Refining Corp.	4/18/68	$300
5. Donald Ingvoldstad	3/12/70	$250
6. Phelps Dodge Refining Corp.	7/10/69	$500
7. Joel Teel	1/15/70	$500
8. Donald Ingvoldstad	3/26/70	$250
9. Joel Teel	11/12/70	$200
10. Donald Ingvoldstad	11/19/70	$25
11. Donald Ingvoldstad	11/19/70	$25
12. Note Herman Cochner Warrant	9/19/68 (outstanding)	

The court was told that Ingvoldstad was a fourth and fifth offender and that the maximum fine of $1,000 should be imposed on each count. According to the intradepartmental file:

> Judge Lawrence Gresser stated that Corporation Counsel should submit a petition to the defendant (who is a multiple offender) in advance so that he can prepare his case properly before appearing in court. He stated that this is the procedure in his court, and if the defendant is not notified he is considered a first offender.[18]

The Department claimed that Phelps Dodge, which is one of 33 known major industrial polluters, was properly served. A former City EPA attorney assigned to air pollution, Douglas Kramer, commented on the Phelps Dodge case: "I know all about it. They threatened to leave the city. I, too, was getting that bull about industry being a minor [air pollution] problem."[19]

Consolidated Edison Cases

As of April 12, 1971, the court record of Consolidated Edison, including all of its 15 plants, was as follows:

	Summonses served	Convictions	Withdrawn by the city	Dismissed by the city	Pending adjustments	Fines collected
1963	5	5	—	—	—	$ 125
1964	7	7	—	—	—	275
1965	16	15	1	—		1,175
1966	15	5	2	8	—	800
1967	24	13	3	8	—	1,575
1968	12	1	3	8	—	250
1969	61	10	5	11	35	425
1970	197	6	8	31	152	210
Subtotal	337	62	22	66	187	$4,835
Average fine per conviction: $78						
1971	22	—	9	—	13	$25 (in a carryover of a 1969 case)

The adjournment and dismissal rate is high, according to Pieratti, because "Con Ed rarely pleads guilty. I can't remember when—they always go for a trial (that means lots of adjournments) and they win them. They walk in with their lawyers and staff people and charts. They even use audiovisual aids and they clobber corporation counsel. . . . The record's a beauty, isn't it—$25 by spring 1971 on a 1969 case!"[20]

Con Ed's individual plant record is similar to its general record. An example dating back several years ago is particularly interesting because it was heavily publicized in the press and at the City Council, with action promised.[21] As first reported by Abel Silver of the New York Post, the story is as follows:

The Consolidated Edison Co. is still being tried as a first offender even though it has been convicted 32 times since 1963 for polluting the air. . . .

A company official yesterday was fined only $100— the maximum permissible for a first offense. Under the City's new stronger air pollution law, a three-time repeater could receive up to a $1,000 fine and six months in jail. As the law is now applied, action is directed against the specific plants emitting pollution, and the individual deemed to be in charge of the particular plant is held accountable.

Thus, several violations could be charged to one plant, but if a different individual is in charge at the time of every violation, each case could be considered a first offense punishable by a $100 fine. Likewise, a supervisor with a record of violations at other plants would still be a first offender should a complaint be made against him after his transfer to a new station. . . .

The offense tried before Criminal Court Judge Jacoby yesterday involved the company's generating plant at Ravenswood, Queens, largest in the system. Last Oct. 27 an Air Pollution Department inspector observed a stack emitting heavy smoke and served a summons on Paul Keshishian, the general superintendent.

Company officials sought to have the fine levied against the company rather than Keshishian, a Department spokesman said. But they withdrew the request when informed that, because of a prior conviction at the plant in 1965, the company could be fined up to $500 as a second offender.

The Department said Keshishian was a first offender at Ravenswood although he has pollution cases pending against him at other plants. It added: "What's to prevent Con Edison from shifting officials around from plant to plant so they are always first offenders when given a summons?"

Earlier this week Commissioner Heller, accompanied by a high Con Edison official, left for Europe to seek a solution to the air pollution problem here.

The City's Corporation Counsel advises that these summonses be given to an individual, rather than Con Edison, to expedite the cases and because of corporation cannot be jailed. But, it was noted, neither are individuals being locked up.[22]

The New York Times reported that members of the City Council were duly shocked and "moved . . . to close a loophole." Majority Leader Ross was reported as saying: "Something must be done. If a revision of the law is necessary, the council will look into that possibility. . . . It is shocking that at a time when the city is moving on many fronts to implement the council's law—described as the toughest code in the nation—that any 'loophole' would permit continued abuses to the detriment of the public." Former Councilman Low, the author of the 1966 revision to the Air Pollution Control Code, added: "Obviously the system of fines has not achieved the desired results because of the leniency of the judges and the attitude of the company. . . . A Con Edison spokesman said antipollution equipment costing $10 million is being installed at the Ravenswood plant. It is expected to be functioning before mid-summer [1967].[23]

On February 27, 1969, the Department tested the antipollution equipment that was supposed to have been operating in 1967. It was an electrostatic precipitator with dust-collecting efficiency exceeding 99+ for the Ravenswood boiler number 30 which burns oil and coal. Ravenswood boilers numbers 1, 2, 3, and 4, which burn oil, have no electrostatic precipitators, nor have boilers numbers 10 and 20, which burn oil and gas. (The precipitator catches most of the particulate matter emitted by the combustion of both oil and coal.)

But in 1970 the Ravenswood plant still emitted annually, from that one plant alone 973 tons of particulates, 31,374 tons of sulfur dioxide, and 24,240 tons of nitrogen oxides.[24] The figures are supplied by Con Edison and are based on mathematical calculations, not performance. And Hershel Slater of the federal Environmental Protection Agency testified at a public hearing that Con Edison's actual performance "is extremely variable."[25]

Nothing was done by the "shocked" City Council. That the sentencing system continues to operate as before is an open secret. Ravenswood is only one example, and may be not the most shocking. It just happened to be picked up by a reporter.

Other Cases

On May 23, 1969, Roman Ortiz, superintendent of a premises at 1172 Strafford Avenue, the Bronx, pleaded guilty to a smoke emission on April 30, 1969, and was fined $75. The record for that premises then reads:

Date of disposition	Amount of fine
1. 4/22/60	$25
2. 5/24/63	$25
3. 3/5/65	$25
4. 3/18/66	$25
5. 3/18/66	$25
6. 10/28/66	$25
7. 1/13/67	$75
8. 5/23/69	$75

All the defendants were other superintendents, except on one previous offense.[26]

On May 29, 1969, Arnold Goldstein, "agent and vice-president of corporation" owning multiple dwellings located at 144-67-77-87 41st Avenue, Queens, pleaded guilty for failure to have an incinerator operating certificate and was fined $25. The record for that premises then read:

Date of disposition	Amount of fine
1. 1/9/64	$25
2. 3/31/66	$25
3. 10/13/66	$75
4. 11/10/66	$200
5. 5/29/69	$25

The same superintendent was the defendant in all previous cases except the first, when a J. Tanenbaum was the defendant.[27]

In Manhattan on May 21, 1969, Vincent Ferguson, agent for Sutton Associates, pleaded guilty for failure to have an incinerator operating certificate and was fined $25 on each of the 6 counts on the four premises he represented. The record then read:[28]

Address	Date of disposition	Amount of fine
135 E. 54th St.	10/13/55	$25
	1/15/69	$25
	5/21/69	$25
141 E. 56th St.	10/13/55	$25
	7/17/68	$25
	9/4/68	$25
	5/21/69	$25
251 E. 51st St.	10/9/62	$25
	5/21/69	$25
405 E. 56th St.	1/15/69	$25
	5/21/69	$25

One could go on with such examples ad infinitum. Whether multiple dwelling, commercial, industrial, or power source, it's all the same.

It is easy to blame the criminal courts, and some judges do not seem entirely blameless—some judges do ask about the responsible party and have him brought in, but they are exceptions. The senior inspector in charge of the Department's daily court work said, "To understand the criminal court you must understand local politics. Most [judges and defendants] come out of the same clubhouse or real estate office. And as for Corporation Counsel—air pollution is nothing to them."[29] However, a few assistant corporation counsel are considered to "show interest" and are highly regarded by the Department.

Are the court sentencing practices effective? Clearly not. One obvious solution is to abandon criminal court procedures and substitute administrative enforcement. This might help if the administrative

court is properly financed, the hearing officers are competent professional appointments, the administrative court is reasonably honest
and its calendar not overcrowded; and the Department or administrative
court is given the power to impose and enforce penalties. Without
the foregoing, an administrative court may fall prey to the same problems that have plagued the criminal courts.

THE CORPORATION COUNSEL'S ROLE

The New York City Charter provides:

> Except as other provided by law, the corporation counsel
> shall be attorney and counsel for the city and every agency
> thereof and shall have charge and conduct of all the law
> business of the city and its agencies and in which the city
> is interested.[30]

The city's lawyers are the corporation counsel. Although they
do not do every bit of the city's legal business, they certainly maintain
a firm grip on all important business. Most agencies, including the
Air Resources Department, also employ their own house counsel (if
an agency does not have a legal bureau, it employs a lawyer as part
of the agency staff to advise the commissioner). The agency's legal
bureau handles in-house legal matters and corporation counsel appears in court on behalf of the agency.

In addition to court appearances, corporation counsel vigorously
exercises the prerogative of being the ultimate legal "yes-no" man.
The opinions and decisions of the corporation counsel override the
opinions and decisions of an agency's attorneys—there is no question
about who is on top. Thus, the anomaly exists that the lawyers with
specialized experience and commitment to a particular city policy
are prohibited from going to court on behalf of their agency, and thus
are restrained from planning and executing an aggressive legal strategy.[31]

Exactly what are the functions of corporation counsel? Corporation counsel renders advice and must be consulted on legal matters
affecting other agencies, reviews proposed laws and regulations,
advises the heads of agencies or their lawyers upon request, appears
on behalf of agencies in criminal court and recommends the penalty
when there is a plea of guilty (each agency is responsible for the
preparation of the case until it is ready for arraignment, for serving
summonses, and for tracking down defendants who fail to appear).
Corporation counsel also appears on behalf of agencies in civil court,
decides what cases to appeal and handles the appeals—in short, it is

responsible for whatever legal strategy may or may not exist in what the Department views as the battle for air pollution control.[32]

In policy conflicts (that is, interagency conflicts), corporation counsel plays an active role. Its attorneys formulate their own independent opinion after considering the conflicting interests. These opinions, which may differ sharply from those of the principal agency involved, carry greater weight than those of the agency. This in turn creates further conflict between the agency and "its" counsel.[33]

Assistant Corporation Counsel Margolis said, "Environmental Protection Administration lawyers handle only in-house matters. . . . Nothing where an appearance must be made." He added that corporation counsel does not consider an individual agency its client: "Our client is the mayor, not [the Environmental Protection Agency]. . . . We consult with other agencies, but we have our own opinion on how matters should be handled. . . . When asked we so advise the mayor."[34]

Corporation counsel's office is organized like a giant law firm with specialties principally in terms of legal functions. A penalties division is in charge of criminal court prosecutions—four different attorneys handle the day-by-day criminal prosecutions, each permanently assigned to a different borough. A trial division, staffed by a separate group of attorneys, is in charge of most civil litigation. An appeals division, in charge of civil appeals, is staffed by its own specialists. Corporation counsel also has a few substantive specialties, such as antitrust.[35]

Two major problems arise from this kind of organization:
1. Most of corporation counsel's attorneys are generalists in substantive matters and specialists in terms of legal functions, while agency attorneys specialize in substantive areas, such as environmental law, and are generalists in terms of legal functions. Although theoretically this may appear to be perfect dovetailing, in reality it creates conflicts of viewpoint, interest, and intensity.
2. Many attorneys and divisions within corporation counsel handle the cases of a single agency. This causes communication difficulties between the agency staff and "their" attorneys (corporation counsel), and makes impossible the coordination of an overall plan. It also makes it difficult to locate the scattered air pollution control cases. No one attorney seems to know who is handling the other cases, nor what other cases there are.

Corporation counsel's workload and responsibilities are staggeringly large in terms of the total number of cases handled for the city—air pollution control is just a small part. This in itself creates obvious conflicts of viewpoint as to what is important. According to Joseph Coffini, the Department's assistant court officer, "Quick study— that's the way our cases are handled by corporation counsel. We need

our own counsel for court fights. To them air pollution is nothing—
they have so many city departments."36

Air pollution cases are treated no differently than any other kind
of city agency cases. For example, corporation counsel prosecutes
all municipal criminal court cases in a routine manner involving little
preparatory work and no planning. The city uniformly recovers small
fines for municipal violations regardless of the seriousness of the
violation, the particular body of law violated, or the agency involved.
The fault may lie with the preparatory effort, which in turn may be
caused by a work overload, or the fault may lie with the attitude of
an overburdened court system that appears to view municipal violations as minor nuisances. In any event, the present organization of
corporation counsel fails to induce the identification and commitment
of individual attorneys to particular municipal problems.37

The underlying problem may be that corporation counsel is empowered to serve two potentially conflicting masters: (1) the city, as
personified by the mayor, whose job it is to make decisions that bal-
ance conflicting interests, and (2) the agency, whose job it is to carry
out a particular public law. Corporation counsel tends to serve the
former, rather than the latter. Traditionally it has always had close
political ties to the mayor, and identification with general city public
policy certainly has greater appeal and status than acting as advocate
for a single agency. This attitude was succinctly stated by a former
assistant corporation counsel: Maybe [Mayor] Lindsay's program of
associating the disadvantaged with government is more important than
a Mickey Mouse scheme to get landlord compliance."38 Maybe—but
it should not be corporation counsel's job to make those kinds of decisions.

If the city wants well-organized, aggressive air pollution control
enforcement, an absolute prerequisite is the reorganization of legal
functions between corporation counsel and house counsel. One possibility is that an assistant corporation counsel might be placed in charge
of a specialized area, such as air pollution or environmental protection.
The attorney could continue to work out of the corporation counsel's
office, but he would have total responsibility for the Department's
legislation, regulations, and cases. He would be the commissioner's
attorney and coordinate legal strategy with Department policy, as is
done in New Jersey. Or the Department's attorneys (and attorneys
for other agencies) could be enpowered to appear in court and given
total responsibility, with corporation counsel rendering advice only
when requested. Or an administrative court with power to impose
and enforce penalties could be established. The bulk of the legal
business would then be conducted at the administrative level, since
appeals usually are limited to arbitrary and capricious decisions.
The appeal work would continue to be handled by corporation counsel.

The proposed New York City solution embraces none of the above proposals. An administrative court will be formed, but without the power to enforce penalties. An alleged violator will be fully entitled to a de novo legal trial on all issues, including the issue of penalties, at the discretion of the court, and court appearances will continue to be handled by corporation counsel. Under this system, it will be difficult to retain "strong" house counsel—experienced persons associated with decision-making and planning—since such persons are not attracted to emasculated positions.39

It appears that corporation counsel has little conception of what the air pollution problem is all about. If air pollution is to be controlled, it will not be by low-keyed conservative lawyers who are trying to represent conflicting city interests, but by an aggressive, imaginative, fighting staff attached directly to the Department.

NOTES

1. Code Criminal Procedures, Sec. 150 (1); N.Y.C. Criminal Court Act, Sec. 57 (1); N.Y.C. Adm. Code, ch. 57, sec. 1403.2-15.25 (criminal penalties), sec. 1403.2, 15.01 (b) (5) (6) (7) (civil penalties) (1971).

2. People ex rel. Mertig v. Johnson, 186 Misc. 1041, 62 N.Y.S. 2d 427 (Sup. Ct., 1946); Code Criminal Procedure, Sec. 150 (1) and (2); N.Y.C. Criminal Court Act, Sec. 57 (7); conversations with court clerks in 1969 and 1971; interviews with former Inspector Roberts in charge of court matters from December 1968 through April 1969.

The procedure for air pollution warrants is described by the Community Service Society of New York in Code Enforcement for Multiple Dwellings in N.Y.C. as follows:

> The case load for the warrant officers averages about 70. A case load for Part 6 may be as high as 200 or as low as 20. The warrant officer's procedure usually follows this pattern:
> 1. he sends a form letter to the defendant's address as given by a department, notifying the defendant of the issuance of a warrant;
> 2. he tries to reach the defendant by telephone;
> 3. he visits the defendant's last address known to the department;
> 4. he notifies the Telephone Company, the Post Office and Con Edison of the warrant and requests information on accounts and the address and phone number of the defendant.

If a person is not located within two months, the
warrant is returned to the court with a report of what the
warrant officers have done. The report has been previously checked by the warrant officers' supervisor. The
warrant is stamped "unable to locate" and is filed. There
is no time limit within which the warrant must be exe-
cuted; if the defendant comes in months later, a file is
checked for outstanding warrants and when an open case
is found it is reactivated.

The warrant procedure also is described in unsigned intradepartmental memo dated June 5, 1970.
   3. People v. Perfecto Chemical Co., 123 Misc. 443, 206 N.Y.
Supp. 15 (Sup. Ct. 1924); interviews with Pieratti and Incristo, spring
1971.
   4. Unsigned intradepartmental memo dated June 5, 1970. The
memo reads in part as follows:

Warrants are sewer service. Outstanding Court
cases as of 6/1/70 indicates there are 2,329 outstanding
court cases of which 599 are warrants.

Cases	Outstanding	Warrants
Man.	659	156
Bklyn.	509	141
Bronx	460	151
Queens	688	67
Rich.	13	84

There are about 150-170 bench warrants outstanding in the five boroughs.

   5. Intradepartmental memos entitled "Summons Data" from
Anthony Incristo to Joseph Schechter, dated March 4, 1971, and "Court
Case Study" from Incristo to Harold Romer dated July 28, 1969. The
latter memo states in part:
   It appears that the main block is that 66% of all
cases presented in court do not resolve and must be
carried over either on the warrants list or adjournments.
   I have prepared a comparative schedule showing the
new cases versus the total cases presented in court.
These figures are in addition to our stockpile of dead
warrant cases, which at present exceeds approximately
1,000.

6. Interview with Pieratti, January 6, 1971.

7. Interview with Pieratti, April 12, 1971.

The problem of serving N.Y.C. landlords is principally caused by two factors:

- New York is unique in having the overwhelming bulk of its housing owned by remote corporations. In other cities nearly all housing consists of private homes or small owner-occupied multiple dwellings.

- An additional major difficulty is that New York does not re- quire registration of title to real property (Real Property Law, Art. 12 & 9). If an owner chooses to take a risk on the security of his title, he is under no obligation to disclose his ownership through registration of the deed. This identity of the responsible party is a summons serving problem. The Multiple Dwelling Law and Code Sec. 325 and Administration Code, Sec. D26-3.1 require registration of the owner, but failure to register does not impair title; it is punishable in the same manner as other housing violations, and subjects the property to a penalty of $250.

8. Interview with Pieratti, spring 1971.

9. N.Y.C. Adm. Code, ch. 57, sec. 1403.2-15.25 (criminal pen- alties), sec. 1403.2-15.01 (b) (5) (6) (7) (civil penalties) (1971).

10. Rules of the Criminal Court of the City of New York, Rule 1 (establishing parts in each borough and authorizing administrative judge to establish subparts). See 1963 Criminal Court citations. Other city agencies prosecuting in Part 6 include buildings health, fire, water supply, gas and electricity, and sanitation.

11. Interview with Coffrini, April 12, 1971; interviews with Roberts from December 1968 to April 1969; interview with Irving Gerstein, spring 1971.

12. New York Post, May 13, 1971.

13. Interview with Pieratti, January 8, 1971; interview with Coffrini, April 12, 1971.

14. Suspended sentences, Code Crim. Proc. Sec. 47a; People ex rel. Forsyth V. Court of Sessions, 141 N.Y. 288, 36 N.E. 386 (1894).

15. N.Y.C. Adm. Code, ch 41, sec. 894-3.0 (1966), amended ch. 57, sec 1403.2-15.25 (1971).

16. According to an intradepartmental memo dated February 4, 1971, from Anthony Incristo, and Joseph Schechter, "our records do indicate that there is an average fine of $35 for the resolved cases. . . . Smoke emission cases incline to raise the average fine due to the occasional high fines of $500 for repeated (9.03) offenders, while Local Law 14 cases are usually fined $25." A humorous note on how pitifully low fines can be is the following memo (concerning a very misinformed judge) from Joseph Coffrini, assistant court officer, to Anthony Palermo, chief enforcement officer, dated May 29, 1970:

On May 28, 1970, in Queens Criminal Court Judge
Gresser was presiding. Assistant Corporation Counsel
Mullaney was in attendance representing the People. On
two cases involving Harold Childs, 210-50 41st Avenue,
Queens-Section 11.19—Violation date May 1, 1970—broken
auxiliary gas burner on incinerator. A $10.00 fine was
imposed. A $10.00 fine was imposed on Woodside Ter-
race Inc., 55-05 Woodside Avenue, Queens—violation date
November 12, 1969, 892-4.3—no operating certificate for
refuse burning equipment.

Assistant Corporation Counsel Mullaney and my-
self objected vigorously to the above fines. We informed
Judge Gresser that the minimum fine of $25.00 for the
first offense should be given to the defendant. Judge
Gresser stated that there was no minimum fine in our
Code for a first offense.

A recess was called by Judge Gresser. Mr.
Mullaney went into conference with the Judge to explain
Section 894-3.0 of the Air Pollution Control Code (and the
set fines). After conferring with Judge Gresser, Mr.
Mullaney notified me that he had clarified the situation,
which was better understood by Judge Gresser.

17. Coffrini, spring 1971.
18. Intradepartmental file (undated).
19. Interview with Kramer, April 9, 1971.
20. Interview with Pieratti, April 12, 1971.
21. See, for example, New York Post, March 10 and 11, 1967,
World Journal Tribune, March 10, 1967; Long Island Press, March 10,
1967; and New York Times, March 11, 1967.
22. New York Post March 10, 1967.
23. New York Times, March 11, 1967.
24. Ibid.
25. Intradepartmental report dated March 1971.
26. Ibid.
27. Ibid.
28. Ibid.
29. Interview with Coffrini, April 12, 1971.
30. N.Y.C. Charter, Sec. 394 (a). Also see Charter Sec. 395
which provides that "The corporation counsel may assign an assistant
or assistants to any agency and or officer of agency, unless herein
otherwise especially provided, shall have or employ any attorney or
counsel (except that an officer may employ counsel to defend himself
against personal liability)." In practical interpretation, the section
merely restricts the employment of counsel in litigation.

31. A brief history of the Air Resources Department house counsel is of interest. The Department had no legal bureau until 1970. For many years one lawyer was employed as part of the staff. After his retirement, the Department decided that to have a decent enforcement program it needed "strong" house counsel. Salaries were raised to a competitive level (the old salary was about $15,000) and John Kaufman was hired. He stayed about a year (1968-69), then Steven Salup was hired. He also stayed about a year (1969-70). Then Neil Fabriant was appointed chief counsel of EPA and he employed two lawyers to work on air pollution control—Bob Czeisler and Douglas Kramer. They also lasted about a year (1970-71). Kaufman, Fabriant, Kramer, and Czeisler all left for different reasons, but they all said, in individual interviews, that they felt frustrated and unable to do a job under the present set up.

The following story by Bob Czeisler, former City EPA attorney assigned to air pollution, illustrates the relationships between corporation counsel and the city agencies:

When the proposed Code was submitted to Milton Weinberg last fall (1970) he wanted to rewrite it starting with the numbering system. [In 1964 the Columbia University Legislative Drafting Research Fund revised the Code and changed the numbering system in order to make it easier to use and to permit necessary expansion. The older Code had adopted the Administrative Code numbering system, which is notoriously senseless and difficult to use.] He wanted to go back to the Administrative Code numbering system, rewrite the Code, then resubmit it back to EPA, then back to him, then to the other agencies affected, then to City Council. It was going to take forever.

We got [Norman] Redlich [first assistant corporation counsel] to stick up for the numbering system and he got [Lee J.] Rankin [the corporation counsel] in on it. And once we won on the numbering we were able to get it [the Code] out of their hands, but with a memo to dump the whole thing with City Council [all previous Air Pollution Control Codes had been enacted as administrative regulation by the Department.] The memo forced the Department to turn the Code over to City Council for enactment, a move with clear political implications although it was decided in a legal memorandum.]

We were forced to work with Weinberg, but he just doesn't believe in air pollution.

[On November 25, 1968, the day of the oral argument in the Oriental Blvd. case, I spoke to Weinberg

about the health effects of air pollution. He said he was
not convinced that air pollution is harmful to health, however, it was reasonable to assume it was and prudent to
pass laws, but the scientific evidence did not convince
him.]

He is a smart lawyer and feels unfairly blamed for
the great delay in the Oriental case, but he is a great
believer in precedence. . . . It's really unbelievable
when we have to deal with other agencies including corporation counsel. The delays involved! We can't get corporation counsel going.

32. Interview with Kramer, April 9, 1971; interview with Czeisler,
spring 1971; interview with Weinberg, January 13, 1971.

33. Ibid.

34. Interview with Margolis, April 26, 1971.

35. Interviews with Gerstein, October 16, 1968, and April 16,
1971.

36. Interview with Coffrini, April 12, 1971.

37. These conclusions are based on observations in court and
conversations with court clerks. Violations of Health Code, Multiple
Dwelling Law, Administration Code, etc., are all treated more or less
the same. Fines are uniformly low (the average is well under $50)
and jail sentences are so rare they are not of significant consideration.

38. Confidential communication.

39. See minutes of executive session of New York City Council,
Committee on Environmental Protection, particularly testimony of
Norman Redlich, first assistant corporation counsel, April 1971.

INDUSTRIAL POLLUTORS

Industrial pollution is treated separately in order to draw attention to the problem. New York is commonly characterized as "a commercial, not an industrial town," but according to the Department of Air Resources, New York contains within its borders "about 20,000 industries . . . An estimated 6,500 of which are emitting particulates of all kinds—gases (including solvents), toxic materials, and smoke from incinerators and boilers."[1]

In other cities the presence of so many industries would characterize a city as industrial. Although industries do not stand out in New York City, their emissions are a greater public hazard than they would be in a smaller city, because of the high population density.

Another myth is that New York City's industries are small. Many are, but not all. The pollutors include, among the more well-known companies, Continental Can, Charles Pfizer, National Gypsum, Pearl Wick Corporate, Phelps Dodge Refining, American Can, Procter and Gamble, National Can, Sun Chemical, Colonial Sand and Stone, Steinway and Sons. All the foregoing companies are on a list of 30 major industrial pollutors based on information required to be supplied by the company to New York State (see Table 2). The Department estimates that large companies contribute about 25 percent of the city's industrial air pollution in the form of particulates "covering a wide range of materials, including liquids in vapor form primarily from solvents, . . . and gases, which are by-products of chemical processes generating sulfur dioxide, acids and gaseous elements or compounds."[2] (The 25 percent does not include industrial smoke emissions from boilers and incinerators.)

The Department began checking the reliability of information supplied by the companies in early 1971. It revised the emission

inventory data of 12 of the 30 pollutors from data already in Department files. In addition, after two months of plant inspection the Department found that 80 percent of the companies were operating illegally.
They had failed to obtain New York City permits for their industrial
equipment, boilers, and incinerators. Needless to say, they also were
violating the city's emission standards.[3]

In addition to industrial emission from within the city's borders,
Staten Island is plagued with emissions from New Jersey's concentra-
tion of chemical and oil refining companies—the largest such concen-
tration in the United States. In the 1930s Staten Island's flower and
vegetable farms were slowly destroyed by air pollutants. As a result,
the federal government conducted its first air pollution investigation
in the New York metropolitan area. Nothing ever came of it, and the
farms disappeared. Today, in Staten Island the issue is not the survival of agriculture but the public health of the rapidly increasing residential population.[4]

Until very recently the Department had no systematic industrial
pollution control program and relied entirely on citizen complaints.
At best, a company was occasionally hauled into criminal court and
fined a minimal amount. It is safe to say that industrial pollution
continues unchecked. For years the Department estimated that industrial pollution accounted for about 2 to 3 percent of the city's total
air pollution, and therefore stated publicly that it was unimportant.

The underplaying of industrial pollution probably also was affected by priorities. In truth, the Department had no idea how many
industrial pollutors there were in the city.[5] A few years ago New York
State enacted an amendment to its air pollution control laws, known
as Part 187, requiring industries throughout the state to submit
environmental rating reports.[6] By the end of 1970, the reports were
in for New York City. Based on these reports, without much further
investigation, it is now estimated that industrial pollution accounts
for about 10 to 15 percent of the city's total air pollution. More important than this percentage is the suspicion that, if industrial pollution
can be controlled, its abatement will have a "big impact on the amount
of particulates in the air." It is also suspected that "industrial emissions are an important ingredient in photochemical smog."[7]

An Industrial Enforcement Task Force was organized on
February 1, 1971 under the guidance of Benjamin C. Radzka, an
engineer. The 1971 operating budget was $60,000 to $65,000, with
the following personnel: Radzka, a second engineer, an assistant
engineer, two inspectors, one clerk, and a student. It was hardly a
formidable army, but that was not Radzka's fault nor the Department's.
He devised a two-year implementation plan requiring a $200,000
annual budget and a staff of approximately 17. He got a full-time
staff of 5 and started the program. By December 1971, he expected

to enlarge the list of 30 major pollutors to about 125, and then go after those companies first.

A company is called a major pollutor if its emissions exceed 25,000 pounds of pollutants per year, or if its emissions are toxic. The top pollutor, solely in terms of weight of emissions, appears to be Continental Can, with an admitted emission of 2 million pounds annually of gaseous solvents. Other companies that are major pollutors include Asbeka Asbestos Machining Corporation, which emits 2,100 pounds a year of asbestos particulates (highly toxic); National Lead Company which emits an estimated 82,000 pounds annually of lead particulates (also toxic); and a dozen or so other companies that each emit, by their own admission, between 100,000 and 600,000 pounds annually of particulates and solvent (see Table 2).8

The task force's first job was to survey and audit the pollutors. New York State's list requires substantial additional work. Some of the addresses were found to be inaccurate, some industries had discontinued doing business, and about 55 percent of the reporting companies stated that they did not pollute the air. Radzka said,

> One of those "nonpolluting companies" was found to have ten emission sources, so the list must be spot-checked by the type of business. We know some them are lying. We just don't know how many. For example, foundries and woodworking outfits have to have an emission. . . . We now figure that maybe 2,500 are the real core of industrial pollution, and of these 125 are really big.

Asked how the pollutors are found since the New York State list admittedly is incomplete and inaccurate, Radzka said,

> They are mostly along the coast line, so as to be near the water. Also we will try to thoroughly inspect zoned industrial areas. . . . The priority I would like to see is to go after the major ones first, so we get a maximum return for our effort, but we are deluged by complaints and specials [mayor specials] which divert us from the big pollutors. . . . Also our people are frequently called to court away from enforcement duties. . . .
> The legal procedure we are using is the service of "orders to show cause why the equipment should not be sealed." That way, we get a hearing [the hearing is informal]. The Agency may seal [which is most unlikely] but it may not penalize. What we hope to do is stimulate them by the threat to seal. Maybe we'll get 25 percent compliance that way. About 50 percent appeared to be

TABLE 2

Major Industrial Pollutors in New York City

Company and Location	Type of Manufacturing	Number of Employes	Number of Emission Sources	Particulate Emission (pounds per year)	Com-plaint Record
Continental Can 50-02 55th. Ave., Queens	metal cans	600	39	2,000,000 (gas, solvent)[a]	light
Charles Pfizer & Co. 11 Bartlett St., Brooklyn	pharmaceuticals	2,200	28	41,000 (solids) 518,000 (gas, solvent)	no file
National Gypsum Co. Barry Oak Pt. Ave. Bronx	gypsum products	186	22	494,000 (solids)[a]	light
Sun Chemical Corp 441 Tompkins Ave. Staten Island	pigments	400	4	285,000 (solids)[a]	no file
Pearl-Wick Corp. 27-50 First St. Long Island City, Queens	bath room	200	45	22,000 (solids) 448,000 (gas, solvent)[a]	no file
Phelps-Dodge Refining Corp. 42-02 56th. Rd. Maspeth, Long Island	wire reclamation	800	10	248,000 (solids)[a]	heavy
American Can Co. 43rd. St. and 2nd Ave. Brooklyn	containers, metal, glass, paper	Relocated to Greenwich, Conn., January 1, 1971	18	236,000 (gas, solvents)[a]	light
Colonial Sand & Stone Pier 18 Staten Island	concrete cement mixes	3,000 throughout New York City.	4	174,600 (solids)[a]	no file
Nassau Smelting & Re-fining Co. Nassau Pl. Tottenville, Staten Island	wire reclamation	600	22	173,000 (solids)[a]	heavy
Brenner Sawdust & Co. 544 Stewart Ave. Brooklyn	sawdust processing	14	unknown	120,000 (solids)[b]	no file
Brooklyn Moulding Co., Inc. 1380 Randall Ave. Bronx	mouldings (wood)	20	unknown	110,000 (solids)[b]	light
Proctor & Gamble Port Ivory Staten Island	detergents	1,500	35	105,000 (solids)[a]	light
Taylor & Co., Inc. 680 Morgan Ave. Brooklyn	foundry	250	7	100,000 (solids) 28,000 (solids)[a]	medium
National Can Corp. 4-40 44th Dr. Long Island City, Queens	tin cans	700	8	92,500 (gas, solvents)[a]	light
U.S. Gypsum Co. 561 Richmond Terrace Staten Island	gypsum products	600	41	88,000 (solids)[a]	none
Columbia Asphalt Corp. 127-50 Northern Blvd., Flushing, Queens	asphalt	10	2	60,000 (solids)[a]	none

Company and Location	Type of Manufacturing	Number of Employes	Number of Emission Sources	Particulate Emission (pounds per year)	Complaint Record
Industrial Plywood Co., Inc. 182-20 Liberty Ave. Queens	paneling plywood	65	unknown	56,000 (solids)[b]	light
Hochberg Bros. & Shan, Inc. 386 3rd Ave. Brooklyn	fixtures (store)	300	9	54,265 (solids)[a]	medium
Steinway & Sons Steinway Pl. Queens	pianos	500	unknown	54,000 (solids)[b]	medium
Belmont Smelting & Refining Wks. 330 Belmont Ave. Brooklyn	metal reclamation	100	2	50,000 (solids)[b]	light
Jacob Froehlich Cabinet Works 560 Barry St. Bronx	woodworking	100	unknown	45,000 (solids)[b]	light
Commercial Smelting & Refining 184-212 Maspeth Ave. Brooklyn	metal (copper) reclamation	20	2	39,000 (solids)[b]	medium
Miller-Hoff Parlor Frame Co. 27 Skillman St. Brooklyn	wood frames	108	unknown	29,000 (solids)[b]	heavy
Boro Kitchen Cabinets Co. 56-06 Cooper Ave. Brooklyn	Cabinets	80	unknown	25,000 (solids)[b]	none
Scottex Corp. 625 Wortman Ave. Brooklyn	textiles mills	160	2	odors (gas)[a]	no file
Van Iderstine Co. 37-30 Review Ave. Queens	meat processing, rendering	100	7	odors (gas)[a]	heavy
J. R. Elkins, Inc. 518 Gardner Ave. Brooklyn	aluminum reclaiming	55	1	remove equipment violations	heavy
National Lead Co. 85 Jay St. Brooklyn	metals	35	1	82,000 (solids, lead)[c]	no record
Asbeka Asbestos Machining Corp 2324 McDonald Ave. Brooklyn	asbestos products	32	3	2,100 (solids, asbestos)[a]	no file
Welbilt Corp. 57-18 Flushing Ave. Queens	stoves	1,090	5	10,000[b]	heavy

[a]Based on available environmental rating report.
[b]Based on emission inventory estimates (modified).
[c]No emission data available.

stimulated by the letters we sent out. We aren't going the criminal court route. It doesn't work. . . .

Yes, the program is definitely getting off the ground. How far it will go is questionable. Dealing with the hard-core pollutors is the tough part.[9]

Deputy Commissioner Hart has adequately summarized the city's posture on industrial pollutors by saying, "This is admittedly a weak area."[10]

SULFUR CONTENT OF FUELS

Sulfur emissions can be controlled by burning a grade of oil or coal with a low sulfur content, burning desulfurized fuel, or burning natural gas, which contains no sulfur. But each of these fuels has its own pollutants and problems.

Oil and coal emit varying amounts of particulates, nitrogen oxides, and other pollutants. Natural gas does not produce particulate matter, but it does have a high nitrogen content. Oil can be burned with automatic equipment to insure a low particulate emission, while coal is burned in household burners with manually controlled equipment, thus resulting in high particulate and volatile emissions. Coal is burned "automatically" in powerhouse boilers, but if a boiler will smoke if it is overloaded or underloaded (not uncommon occurrences in households burning coal and powerhouse boilers burning coal and oil). Gas can be burned for household use with equipment that will control the nitrogen emission, but such control equipment does not work on huge powerhouse boilers.

Theoretically, high-sulfur fuel could be burned to produce power with the sulfur, (and possibly other pollutants) removed from the boiler stack and sold, for sulfur is a valuable commodity with many industrial uses. However, such technology is not yet commercially feasible. In 1971 for the first time, Con Edison invested in research and development for the removal of sulfur from the stacks.[11]

Burning a grade of fuel with a low sulfur content does not affect the emission of particulates, which is largely a byproduct of combustion. The amount of particulates emitted is dependent on the efficiency of the combustion process, which in turn depends on the quality and maintenance of the equipment and its operation.

It is well established that sulfur plus particulates can be a deadly combination, particularly with a little humidity thrown in. New York City's air has a high content of both sulfur and particulates. In the early 1960s the federal Department of Health, Education and Welfare (HEW) encouraged the enactment of local regulations to limit the sulfur content of oil and coal, in response to the London smog disasters of 1952 and 1959, and indications were that New York City, which had experienced a severe air pollution incident on October 20, 1963, was headed in the same direction. Since there was no easy way to limit the particulate "content" of oil and coal used for household and power purposes, the push was to control the sulfur content of the fuel.

In 1963 HEW mathematically calculated that in order for New York City to achieve an air quality of 0.1 parts per million of sulfur dioxide on a 24-hour average, the sulfur content of both oil and coal would have to be strictly controlled. The federal government recommended that number 6 fuel oil, the most heavily used oil, be restricted to no more than 0.75 to 1.0 pounds of sulfur dioxide per BTU (British Thermal Unit) of heat—depending on the kind of fuel burned, different quantities of fuel are needed to achieve one BTU of heat—for example, less oil than coal is required, and less coal than solid waste. HEW also recommended appropriate limits for numbers 2 and 4 oil, and for coal. It calculated that to achieve the minimum quality of air desired, the amount of sulfur dioxide emitted must be reduced by 80 percent, persumably using a 1963 base although no one knew exactly how much sulfur dioxide was emitted then.[12]

Two guideposts were thus established: the sulfur content of the fuel, which was to be regulated by law, and the quantity of sulfur dioxide emitted, which was to be mathematically calculated by the locality annually and reported to HEW. The goal was clear—to get the sulfur content in the air down to a nonharmful level. Since the entire scheme was based on mathematical calculations, and since it was known that weather (humidity, heat, inversions, wind direction), which cannot be controlled, is an important if not decisive variable, no one could be sure that the scheme would work. At the time and under the circumstances, with limited natural gas supplies, it appeared to be a practical plan. HEW was worried, and rightfully so, about an air pollution crisis in New York City, and something had to be done quickly.[13]

During 1963 the Department undertook extensive revision of its rules and regulations with HEW financing. At that time those regulations were New York City's air pollution control law.[14] The Department cautiously recommended a small limitation on the sulfur content of fuel, for example, for number 6 fuel oil a limit of 3.0 pounds of sulfur dioxide per BTU to be reduced to 2.2 over a five-year period. (HEW recommended was 1.0 or less in 1964; New York City achieved 1.0 in 1969.) At the time, the Department considered itself quite daring in recommending any sort of sulfur limitation in fuel. The Department was extremely small (about 100 persons), and it did not have Mayor Wagner's active support (He appeared indifferent rather than opposed, although the Department's budget was cut in 1965).

The Department also feared the wrath of Consolidated Edison and the oil industry. Its fears were warranted. Industry turned out in full force at the public hearings in May 1964 to battle the proposed regulations. Industry was in complete agreement that—as so succinctly stated by Consolidated Edison—"It is our contention that the imposition of the proposed sulfur content limitations is neither practical, economical nor necessary at this time." The National Coal Association threatened to sue, as it had in Los Angeles.[15] Everyone was concerned with supply and cost. The Department and its allies—HEW, Councilman Robert Low, and Dr. Barach of the New York Academy of Medicine— were concerned with public health. And the allies wanted to go much further than the Department did. Dr. Barach wanted to ban sulfur, if possible.[16] That same month Councilman Low introduced a bill into the City Council recommending a 2.5 limit for number 6 fuel oil, to be reduced to 1.0 over a ten-year period. The bill's restrictions were later tightened, incorporated into Local Law 14, and enacted in the spring of 1966.[17]

Enforcement of the law restricting the sulfur content of number 6 fuel oil and coal is undoubtedly "the one program that has gone beautifully."[18] Why? Because it is easy to enforce—it involves dealing with a handful of potential violators, not 70,000 or more.[19] Three companies supply most of the oil to New York City and to Consolidated Edison: Exxon, Hess Amerada, and New England Petroleum (Asiastic Petroleum also supplies a small portion).[20] The companies store the oil in 25 depots, or "farms" as they are called, which are easily spot-checked. One inspector and one lab man sample each depot on a regular basis. More important, enforcement is easy because once the companies comply, the sulfur standard is built into their own production facilities and internal organizational and contractual system. Thus, the law becomes virtually self-enforcing.[21] However, building a legal standard into the companies' internal system means that standards cannot easily be changed. Companies are justified in complaining of the rapid change in standards in recent years. On the other hand, these same companies fight tooth and nail to keep standards to the minimum, thereby increasing their risk of rapidly changing standards.

What about the impact on the air? Although the amount sulfur in the air declined after 1964, the amount at any given time depends more on weather than on the quantity of emissions. On a citywide annual average (which means considerable averaging), New York City's air still contained in 1973 three times more sulfur than the minimum standard recommended by the federal government.

Citywide averages are very deceptive and may show unexpected readings. In 1970, for example, Manhattan, the Bronx, and Brookyln had less sulfur in the air than in 1969, decreases of 15, 5, and 9 percent, respectively, although most fuel is burned in those three boroughs. But Queens and Staten Island, (with 12 percent increases), had markedly more sulfur in the air. Why? Dr. Edward Ferrand, director of Technical Services, said "Wind direction was responsible."22 Hershel Slater, a sulfur dioxide expert from HEW, has said:

> The effect of sulfur dioxide is different according to the season, winds, time of day, etc. For example, in the summer the Bronx get hit heavily with sulfur dioxide because the winds are southerly. Also, Con Ed's emissions are extremely variable. They are highest in the afternoon and the summer emission is very high as compared to other seasons. Sulfur dioxide is normally two or three times greater along the East River. . . . Astoria currently contributes a lot of sulfur dioxide because of its large size and low stacks. . . . The impact of the new proposed sulfur dioxide limits [i.e., 1 percent instead of 3 percent] will have an impact on Con Ed Plants where the emission is elevated, but not on space heating emissions.23

Because averaging the content of the ambient air for the entire city is so deceptive, the federal government requires New York City and all localities to report on their grant applications the reading from the monitoring station with the highest annual average. The reason is public health. People's health is affected by the worst conditions in the city as well as the best, but never by the overall mathematical average. In 1970 the worst New York City station showed 238 micrograms of sulfur dioxide per cubic meter of air—the federally recommended level is 80 micrograms.24

Enforcement and compliance is excellent. Impact on the air is poor, and in some ways unexpected. Where do we go from here? The code (revised in the fall of 1971) proposes even stricter sulfur limitations. However, Ken Johnson, regional director for the Federal Environmental Protection Agency, said the proposed limitations were not strict enough to comply with federal air quality standards.25 The government has calculated that full enforcement of the proposed sulfur dioxide standard would result in air containing 0.4 parts per million (annual arithmetic mean) while the proposed national primary air quality standard for sulfur dioxide is 0.03 parts per million and the recommended secondary standard is 0.02 parts per million. These are minimum national standards; it is assumed that areas of high population density will achieve higher standards because of the greater danger to public health. (Even if the proposed sulfur dioxide standard is enacted, the commissioner and the city have already agreed with Con Edison and the real estate industry not to fully enforce from fall 1971 through summer 1972.)26

Ken Johnson also said that "even if we are wrong on our calculations, the city's particulate level is so high that our position is definitely not questionable."[27] But since the danger is sulfur plus particulates, it would appear that the solution is to burn natural gas for household use with proper control equipment and to burn high-grade oil or
coal (with solid waste that may have to be burned anyway) for power
generation, since large-scale equipment can be maintained properly
to control particulate emissions. As for natural gas supplies and
distribution, the power lies not with the Department or the city or
the federal Environmental Protection Administration. It lies with the
oil industry, the Federal Power Commission, and the President acting
in a complex interrelationship of political economics.

A side effect of regulating the sulfur content of number 6 oil
was to contribute to a substantial increase in the use of number 4 oil
(a blend of number 6 with high-quality number 2 oil; the latter is used
in private homes.) Multiple dwellings mostly used number 6 oil and
bituminous (soft) coal. Local Law 14 banned soft coal for space heating, regulated the quality of number 6 oil, and required the upgrading
of boilers using number 6 oil. Some landlords burning number 6 oil
considered it more economical to buy number 4 oil (its price also had
gone up, from 9.5 cents a gallon to 16 cents a gallon) than to buy number 6 at 11 cents a gallon and upgrade the boiler.[28] The law requires
that a permit be obtained to convert from one kind of fuel to another
because substantial equipment changes are required. However,
Pieratti explained,

> Heller made it easy to convert to number 4 from number
> 6 probably to show successful enforcement. All that was
> required is to remove the preheaters [number 6 oil is so
> thick it has to be heated before it will flow] and if the
> equipment had other deficiences we didn't know because
> there was no inspection for that. . . .
> Who converted to number 4? Mostly small build-
> ings that probably had lousy installations. We know the
> blend is good, yet we are getting a lot of smoke. . . .
> Now we are beginning to examine the installations and
> calling for improvements.[29]

Deputy Commissioner Hart said that since the passage of Local
Law 14 about 10 percent of smoke summonses apply to buildings burning number 4 oil. In the past there were no summonses for that grade
of oil. Now, more is used and the quality of the equipment is poor,
so the result is smoke.

ASBESTOS SPRAYING

About 10 years ago, the building trades discovered that spraying fire-retarding material containing asbestos on the supporting beams during construction cut costs by about one-fifth.30 The previous practice was to encase the beams in concrete.

Asbestos is a natural substance long familiar to man as an excellent fire-retarding material, but it is also a well-documented carcinogenic substance.31 New Yorkers gained first-hand knowledge of this new "economic" trade practice when they found themselves showered by "asbestos snows." The most well-known instances were the "snows" caused by the asbestos spraying of the General Motors and Gulf and Western buildings in midtown Manhattan. Thousands of New Yorkers of all social classes and ages innocently stood, walked, or drove through these "snows." And since all the sprayed buildings are skyscrapers, the wind carried the asbestos to unknown parts.

Was the New York City Government and the Air Resources Department aware of this clearly hazardous trade practice? Yes. In 1968 a lengthy article published in the New Yorker magazine described the research work of Dr. Irving Selikoff, director of the Environmental Science Laboratory of the Mount Sinai School of Medicine, an expert on the health hazards of asbestos. The article documented cases in South Africa (where asbestos is heavily mined) and the United States of a deadly form of lung cancer (mesothelioma) that is caused only by asbestos, and evidence of other forms of cancer caused by asbestos in the lungs, colon, rectum, and stomach. It made clear that the most insidious aspect of asbestos's effect on health is its delayed reaction. After exposure, an individual feels fine for about 15 to 25 years, the latency growth period. Then he finds himself with a cancer of "unknown" origin or cause. During 1968, Selikoff met with Austin Heller, then commissioner of Air Pollution Control, and the Environmental Protection administrator, Merril Eisenbud, to urge city control of asbestos spraying. Discussions with the construction trade began. "For over a year we tried to get the construction industry to act," Selikoff said. "They said, 'Yes,' and did nothing."32

In 1970, after his reelection as mayor, John V. Lindsay appointed a new commissioner of Air Pollution Control (Robert N. Rickles) and a new Environmental Protection administrator (Jerome Kretchmer), and they in turn appointed new legal counsel. The lawyers, under the leadership of Neil Fabricant, were "shocked" when they learned about the Department's inaction on asbestos spraying. They considered it a health emergency, gave it top priority, and made it their first fight for cleaner air.33 About 150 summonses and many "orders to show cause why the equipment should not be sealed" were served over a period of several months. One company, La Monica, after receiving nineteen summonses and two show-cause orders, sued New York City for infringement on its freedom. The company moved for a preliminary injunction in the New York State Supreme Court to stop the City EPA from enforcing criminal proceedings and administrative sealing procedures on the ground that the Air Pollution Control Code and the orders of the commissioner were unconstitutional.

Judge Riccobono saw the issue as "whether plaintiffs [La Monica] may continue earning their living lawfully as they have in the past, or whether in the interest of protecting the health of millions, including plaintiffs, rules and orders propounded by defendants may make such practices unlawful. The choice here is roughly speaking, between some curtailment of plaintiff's liberties and our very lives." The motion for the injunction was denied on November 18, 1970.[34]

Did this stop asbestos spraying? No. Contracts had been bid and many contractors refused to cooperate. The Department attempted to police about 50 construction sites with just one inspector, or sometimes two. In addition, a spraying, often had been completed by the time the lawyers were informed about it.[35] In April 1970 an article appeared in the Village Voice stating that 5,000 tons of asbestos were to be sprayed (rather than painted) on the beams of the gigantic World Trade Center, which was being built with public funds by a quasigovernmental body—the Port of New York Authority.[36] This proved to be too much—it created a lot of publicity and infuriated and frightened some important people. The asbestos spraying never took place—a substance called Kafco was substituted. The construction industry then undertook general compliance with Department regulations requiring that asbestos spraying be done in an enclosure, floors be vacuumed after the spraying, and so forth.[37] However, the industry continued to use asbestos and refused to give up the cheaper spraying procedure for other, more expensive techniques. Department enforcement by just one inspector continued.

Two problems become apparent:

1. The asbestos regulations did not protect the asbestos sprayers on the city's 225,000 other construction workers. According to Selikoff, "People exposed in an enclosure without an independent outside air source during asbestos spraying will not be alive in 25 years."[38] The regulations, if followed, only help prevent contamination of the community air. They do not protect men working in the enclosure. In addition, Harold Romer, the Department's asbestos expert, has testified that "The workers are working in a cloud of dust—unbelievable conditions. The great majority wear no protection at all because they have to move around a great deal and the masks usually don't fit. All workers are exposed because there is no way to clean up even with a vacuum."[39]

2. The regulations did not protect the general public from the smallest, usually invisible, asbestos particulates, nor did they provide complete protection from the large particulates. The smallest particulates are the most dangerous because they are more likely to enter the deepest recesses of the lungs. Outside of requiring total enclosure of the building being treated with asbestos, there apparently is no way to protect the public from particulates invisible to the naked eye:

Even on jobs ostensibly complying with our orders where there is no visible emission, during clean-up it's impossible to completely vacuum; we see a cloud of large particulates. We therefore conclude that small particulates, which are the most hazardous, are emitted all the time. . . . extremely difficult to control this material.[40]

In addition, Romer said,

Industry has improved its procedures, but we know that they are lax and it is impossible to police them . . . It's tough to get the building industry to do what is necessary. One recent incident—just before Christmas 1970—we got calls that it was snowing asbestos on Sixth and Seventh Avenues in midtown. We traced it to a building construction site on 52nd Street between Sixth Avenue and Broadway. They were violating all of our rules. Torn tarpaulins were permitting asbestos to be airborne. They had left piles of loose asbestos on the lower floors. It was a mess.[41]

However, Dr. Irving J. Selikoff stated, "We have retested where the regulations are enforced, and found that the air around the building contained no more asbestos than the ambient air of N.Y.C."[42] This apparent discrepancy of opinion is caused by the Department's knowledge that the regulations are not carefully followed, and that reliance on Department enforcement is foolhardy considering the seriousness of the hazard.

In fall 1971 the Department proposed a ban on asbestos spraying with substitution of spray materials approved by New York City and a requirement that spraying procedures comply with regulations specified in a then-proposed, since passed, amendment to the Air Pollution Control Code. This amendment contained a key concession to the building trades—namely, the continued legalization of spraying despite the fact that it cannot be policed or controlled. (This was advantageous because the spraying process "saves" money, provided the materials cost about the same as asbestos.) But in Dr. Selikoff's opinion, it would be hazardous to spray any "unknown" substituted material into the open air. Selikoff would prefer to continue using asbestos with safer spraying procedures or other techniques, and tight policing (as apparently is done in England). But the Department, which has greater experience with its own inability to adequately police numerous scattered sites, preferred banning asbestos on the ground that it is known to be a serious public health hazard, and gambling on the safety of the substitute materials. No one proposed that spraying be totally outlawed.[43]

What other sources of asbestos emissions are there in New York City? One factory emits 2,100 pounds of asbestos annually and has continued to operate despite the knowledge of the Department. Selikoff has found asbestos in the recirculated air inside some schools and other newer buildings treated with asbestos. To save money, the air conditioning ducts were not covered with sheet metal. Selikoff said, "I know that uncovered ducts collect fungus, dead rats—when workmen go in to repair, the installation materials may be shaken loose and asbestos gets into the circulating air. The asbestos is now coated with a sealing which is inadequate protection."[44]

In addition, the transportation and warehousing of asbestos is not regulated, and the number of such sources is unknown. Romer, the Department's asbestos specialist, also worries about the demolition of buildings, since a growing number contain asbestos that will be emitted into the open air as demolition dust.

Ironically, the Department officially cites asbestos enforcement as one of its two successful enforcement programs, the other being the sulfur content of fuel. And actually there is truth to the Department's boast when asbestos is compared to its other enforcement programs. On the one hand, the Department behaved aggressively, using its administrative sealing powers as a threat for the first time on a wide scale. But on the other hand, why did it take four years to stop a known carcinogenic public health hazard that may have affected the general population and certainly affected the construction workers? Why does the asbestos factory go on emitting asbestos into the air? Why was only one inspector generally assigned to asbestos detail?[45]

According to Douglas Kramer, the attorney who was in charge of asbestos enforcement for the City EPA:

> The asbestos program is misleading. One inspector—forty or fifty active sites—no follow-up to speak of—by the time it got to my office the spraying was done. And on top of it, City Council, the Building Department, and Corporation Counsel feels that the E.P.A. overstepped itself in the asbestos program. They want to be sure that we don't take the initiative again."[46]

It is abundantly clear from the executive sessions of the City Council's Environmental Protection Committee, which passed an asbestos spraying ban, that the committee intends to amend the law so that in a similar future situation the Department will be powerless to act on its own initiative without a specific explicit mandate. The Department then will have to go to the City Council for new regulations or act under its emergency procedures. Going to the City Council could take years; the emergency powers are defined and set up in such a way as to be unworkable.[47]

In the meantime, the Department's quarterly progress report for the period ending December 31, 1970, described the following "progress" with respect to asbestos:

> Survey of industrial use of asbestos—estimated 70% complete . . . re-survey of plants and warehouses manufacturing asbestos products. Heavy emitters of asbestos dust, first surveyed in the summer of 1968, were revisited to observe and report on improvements. . . . Conference attended at Environmental Science Laboratory of Mt. Sinai School of Medicine on asbestos dust emissions.[48]

In sum, "progress" meant a survey and a conference.

Industry's attitude is well exemplified in the dialogue between Melvin Praeger, past president of the Fireproof Committee of the Construction Association of Metropolitan New York, and City Councilman Eldon Clingan on January 27, 1971, at the public hearings on the proposed air pollution control code—the code passed in fall 1971, includes a ban on asbestos spraying, regulations controlling the spraying of other fireproofing materials, and regulations specifying demolition procedures. The dialogue went as follows:

> PRAEGER: Operation of work within a building should only be supervised by the Department of Buildings. . . . If asbestos is banned then precautionary spraying procedures are unnecessary. . . . We request a time extension on the asbestos banning because 6 to 10 buildings have already been approved for asbestos spraying, changing the materials to be sprayed will take a year and cost $8 to $10 thousand in tests, and because practical knowledge is not the regulations—they will cost delay and money.
>
> CLINGAN: When did industry begin to comply with spraying regulation?
>
> PRAEGER: During the past year and one quarter we have cut out the carelessness and made sure the spraying is done in an enclosure. Prior to this there was some carelessness, but not by the big contractors.

CLINGAN: Weren't Gulf and Western [building] and World Trade Center handled by big contractors?

PRAEGER: When working on a high rise exposed to weather you are bound to get emissions of particulate matter.

CLINGAN: Until Rickles' moratorium [spring 1970] the contractors were paying no attention.

PRAEGER: In my opinion the companies have gone overboard to protect the public.

CLINGAN: Why have the companies taken precautionary measures?

PRAEGER: To prevent the emission of asbestos.

CLINGAN: Because it's a threat to public health?

PRAEGER: Nothing has been proven. Evidence has come from observations in different industries. Spraying on the fireproofing material, which has taken the place of concrete, is economical and is therefore necessary in a period of rising costs.

CLINGAN: The action of the construction industry may have led to a probability of a cancer epidemic in this City in about 20 years. For you to argue economics is not germane when weighing against the possibility of a cancer epidemic. What about asbestos floating around in building air conditioners?

PRAEGER: Now it's not possible because we coat the asbestos.

CLINGAN: Dr. Selikoff disagrees: "We are not sure that coating or sealing is enough protection."

PRAEGER: No responsible contractor would use a material that would harm his workers because it's inhuman and uneconomical.

CLINGAN: If supporting beams were covered with concrete rather than sprayed it would cut emissions by 70-80%?

PRAEGER: Yes.[49]

NOTES

1. Benjamin Radzka, "Plan to Control Industrial Air Pollutants" (mimeo.; intradepartmental report, February 22, 1971). Of the 20,000 industries in New York City, only 5,000 have admitted that they are polluting. The 6,500 figure is the Department's estimate of the number of actual pollutors. The report states that "Industrial plants located in the City limits include asphalt producers, textile finishers,

78

renderers, foundries, chemical plants, woodworking, food processing, pharmaceuticals, building materials, smelting and refining, metals reclamation, consumer goods manufacturing, appliances, jewelry processing, plating, dry cleaning, etc. to name a few."

The Low Committee estimated the number of industries contributing to air pollution in 1965 at about 8,000. The committee's estimate and analysis of industrial pollution contributed significantly to the myth that industrial pollution was insignificant. See the Interim Technical Report of the Special Committee to Investigate Air Pollution (M-970), Air Pollution in New York City (mimeo.; Council of the City of New York, June 22, 1965), pp. 46-48.

The Low Committee Report gives the following estimate of the total number of manufacturing establishments in New York City:

Industry	Total number of establishments
Food and kindred products	1,508
Paper and allied products	672
Chemicals and allied products	889
Petroleum and coal products	—
Rubber and miscellaneous plastic products	446
Stone, clay and glass products	467
Primary metals industries	232
Fabricated metal products	1,957
Machinery (excluding electrical)	1,255
Electrical machinery	935
Total	8,371

The low Committee described industrial pollution as follows:

It was not possible, in this study, to estimate process emissions for each of the many industries located in New York City. Rough calculations have been made for only the few industries described below which indicate that although they could cause local nuisances in the vicinity of the individual plants, their contribution to the overall pollution emission for the City would be small. This data is not included in any of the discussion or tables.

There are 13 asphalt batching plants in New York City, including four City-owned plants, having a total capacity of 6,100 tons per day. Control in these asphalt plants consists primarily of cyclones and scrubbers. In three of these plants, electrostatic precipitators are used as secondary collectors in place of scrubbers.

There are 26 major coffee roasters in the city, producing a total of between 105,000 and 110,000 tons of coffee per year, and 10 small roasting plants.

New York City has one large ferrous foundry with two cupolas, producing about 25 tons of iron castings per day, and a medium-sized ferrous foundry with one cupola producing about four tons of castings per day. Both foundries employ afterburners for fume control.

There are two large brass and bronze foundries, one processing 35 tons of metal per day and the other processing ten tons of metal per day. There are also 79 commercial, non-ferrous foundries handling a total of 20 tons of metal per day. The larger foundries have bag houses for the control of dust and fumes. However, the smaller non-ferrous foundries, employing less than ten men, usually do not employ control equipment. . . .

New York City also has several sugar refineries and bulk drug manufacturing plants. The City is justly famous for the great amount of construction and demolition of buildings that is constantly going on. In 1963 over 8,000 new buildings were completed, at an estimated cost of close to 900 million dollars. As the largest seaport in the nation, New York City has numerous coal and oil burning ships in its harbor at all times. There are four large breweries in New York, having an aggregate 1964 capacity of over nine million barrels a year. All these myriad activities can give rise to dust, smoke, fume and odor and add to the overall pollution burden of the City."

Note, the present estimate is about 20,000 industrial pollutors. That estimate does not include such important commercial pollutors as dry cleaning establishments (solvents) and gasoline service stations and garages (evaporation of gas).

2. Radzka, "Plan," op. cit.

3. Interview with Radzka, April 21, 1971. On the estimate of 80 percent licensing illegalities, see the intradepartmental memo from Benjamin Radzka to Commissioner Robert Rickles, "Industrial Enforcement Task Force" (mimeo.; March 16, 1971). Between its activation on February 1 and the March 16 report, the task force surveyed 36 companies and found 29 violating the code and only 7 complying. The report states:

Violations included four major types, as follows:

1. Failure to file plans, obtain permits, and certificates of operation on new industrial process installations.

2. Failure to file environmental rating reports.

3. Failure to upgrade oil burners as required by Local Law 14, or to complete work described in the application.

4. Excessive emission of air contaminants (including odors) detrimental to persons or property.

The number of violations per company averaged between 2 and 3, and was distributed as follows:

Violations per company	No. of Companies
1	6
2	10
3	9
4	2

Twenty-seven industrial directives were issued, 2 violation notices, no summonses. At least 13 companies advised that they have retained professional services to effect compliance with the Code.

The annual industrial fuel consumption in the City is approximately 400,000 tons of bituminous coal, 202 million gallons of number six oil, 160 million gallons of number four oil, 50.4 million gallons of number two oil and 22 billion cubic feet of natural gas. No data could be obtained to determine which portion of fuel was used for space heating and which portion for process use. It has been assumed that all of the coal was used for space heating, and that use of oil and natural gas was equally divided between space heating and process use.

When asked whether industrial boilers and incinerators are included in the Department's Local Law 14 upgrading statistics, Radzka said: "To the degree they were not reported, they aren't in the statistics." This is not unimportant because Radzka found 80 percent of boilers and incinerators were unlicensed, so presumably the number of pollutors is even higher. Radzka, April 21, 1971.

4. Interview with Megonnel, March 9, 1971.

5. Interviews with Pieratti, April 12, 1971, and Radzka, April 21, 1971.

6. Public Health Law, Sec. 1271, 1276 (Part 187).

7. Interview with Ferrand, April 21, 1971.

8. Radzka, "Plan," op. cit.

9. Radzka, April 21, 1971. A letter from Commissioner Robert Rickles to the New York Times, April 24, 1971, stated, "a new industrial pollution task force has opened a drive on the 6,000 industrial pollutors in the City. Over 60 notices to seal equipment have been issued."

10. Interview with Hart, December 21, 1970.

11. New York Post, May 18, 1971, p. 12.

12. Letter from Robert A. Low, New York City Councilman to Maureen Neuberger, U.S. Senator, June 22, 1964; letter from V. J. MacKenzie, Chief, Division of Air Pollution, to Senator Neuberger, August 8, 1964.

13. Interview with Ferrand, April 21, 1971; Blade and Ferrand, "Sulfur Dioxide Air Pollution in New York City: Statistical Analysis of Twelve Years," APCA Journal 19 (1969), p. 873.

14. N.Y.C. Air Pollution Control Code, sec. 13.03 (1963) amended N.Y.C. Adm. Code, ch 57, sec. 1403.2-13.03 (1971).

15. Testimony by Consolidated Edison and the National Coal Association at the public hearing to consider the proposed Air Pollution Control Code, May 1964.

16. Testimony by Dr. Barach, New York Academy of Medicine, at Public Hearings on Proposed Air Pollution Control Code in May 1964:

> Most of you perhaps do not know that pulmonary emphysema is perhaps the most common cause of disability of men, and next to that is coronary disease and the Selective Service Act. The reason that people are short of breath is because the airway is very narrowed for one thing. . . . The slightest degree of sulfur dioxide in the atmosphere causes this swelling in the airway. It's been proven experimentally in Kingley by Sims and Praven and others that sulfur dioxide in the atmosphere causes bronchial spasms, and asthmatic response. . . .
>
> Now gentlemen, bronchial spasms have never been precipitated in any degree by cigarette smoke. . . . At no time can an individual inhale sulfur dioxide in concentrations say of 1.4 parts per million without showing signs of increased, or an increase in resistance to the flow of air. . .
>
> We have evidence clinically, we have evidence experimentally, there is now evidence immunologically that sulfur dioxide is not only an irritant but it is a dangerous hazard to health. . . .
>
> Finally there is this business of lung cancers. We don't know exactly just what causes lung cancer. We do know there is an association with lung irritants. . . .

We know in all the responsible studies that people exposed
to air pollutants have an incidence of lung cancer twice that
of people who are not so exposed. . . .

The immediate thing is we have a possible catas-
trophe in New York City as a result of sulfur dioxide and
an unquestionable situation in which sulfur dioxide exacer-
bates, shortens the breath of patients with pulmonary
emphysema.

At the hearings, on the subject of oil supply:

Ben Linsky: "Availability of low sulfur oil unknown. Information part of trade secrets. The fuel becomes available as laws
are passed, so shortages are questionable."

Schwartz of Consolidated Edison: "We will need less oil and
coal in the future despite increased power demands because we are
improving our internal procedures to utilize what we have more
efficiently."

"Lots of low sulfur oil will be available by 1975 when the de-
sulfurization plants are in full operation." Hearings May 21, 1971.

On oil costs, it is interesting to quote from a statement by
Councilman Low at the public hearing when the first restriction on
the sulfur content of fuel was proposed by the Department:

But, if the industry is going to balk and resist every step
of the way and I notice it has in the statements presented
here today, it may end up with even more restrictive
measures. Now, without trying to be cute I say that the
industry is throwing out a smoke screen today when it
indicates it's going to increase the cost of this number
six fuel oil by fifty percent if we require tolerable limits
of sulphur content.

If you read the journal of commerce you will see the
fluctuation of price between the premium grade six and
the residual six which has the high sulfur content and the
fluctuation is about a half a cent to a cent a gallon. This
doesn't mean that you're going to increase your cost of
fuel by fifty percent by any means.

I would suspect that if this were spread over the
consumers of the city it would amount to pennies or
something like that a year, not fifty percent of the fuel
bill.

But by 1971 the industry increased the cost of premium number
6 not by 50 percent but by 100 percent (5.5 cents a gallon to 11 cents
a gallon).

17. N.Y.C. Adm. Code, ch. 41, sec. 893-1.0 (1966) amended ch 57 sec. 1403.2-13.03 (1971).

18. Ferrand, April 21, 1971.

19. Interview with Conrad Simon, July 28, 1969, and spring, 1971.

20. Ferrand, April 21, 1971.

21. Testimony of Fred Hart at the executive session of the New York City Council, Committee on Environmental Protection, May 14, 1971; Interview with Rickles, spring 1971. It might be noted that Commissioner Rickles said in a speech that each depot was checked quarterly; Deputy Commissioner Hart said each depot was checked once a month, and from the sample taken about 60 tests were run monthly.

22. Interview with Ferrand, April 21, 1971.

23. Testimony of Hershel Slater, public hearings on proposed revision of air pollution control law, New York City Council, Committee on Environmental Protection, February 3, 1971.

24. Information supplied by Ken Johnson, federal Environmental Protection Agency regional director.

25. Interview with Johnson, May 1971.

26. On nonenforcement of the proposed Code: confidential communications heard at executive session, of New York City Council Committee on Environmental Protection, May 14 and May 21, 1971.

27. Johnson, May 1971. At the public hearing on proposed revision of air pollution control law, New York City Council, Committee on Environmental Protection, February 3, 1971, EPA Regional Director Ken Johnson testified that the "Only way to achieve annual sulfur dioxide standard, only way it can be done is by conversion to natural gas, at least for Manhattan.... We must go to natural gas."

28. Interview with Hart, December 21, 1970.

29. Interview with Pieratti, spring 1971. N.Y.C. Adm. Code, ch 57, sec. 1403.2-13.03 (c) (1971) now regulates sulfur content of number 4 fuel oil.

30. Testimony on asbestos at public hearing on proposed revision of air pollution control law, February 25, 1971, New York City Council, Committee on Environmental Protection.

31. Interview with Romer, January 15, 1971; testimony of Dr. Irving Selikoff, Executive Session, New York City Council Committee on Environmental Protection, February 25, 1971. On the amount of asbestos in the air and its effect on health, Dr. Selikoff's testimony was as follows:

Question: What is happening with asbestos in New York City's ambient air? Is it the same? Getting less?

Answer: No way to know. The first sample was taken a little over a year ago by our laboratory. We expect asbestos in the air to come down.

Question: Is there a level of asbestos that is trivial?

Answer: No safe minimum level has been established. What we know is that we have looked at post-mortems for 50 consecutive months and found asbestos in every person although these people did not die of an asbestos disease. Our guess is that it takes a fair amount of asbestos. . . . Also cigarette smoking is an important variable. In January 1963 we started watching 370 male asbestos workers of 25 to 30 years of age. Among the 283 cigarette smokers we have now seen 41 lung cancers where we would normally expect 4 lung cancers, while among the 87 noncigarette smokers we found one lung cancer which is exactly what we can expect. We therefore calculate the combination of asbestos plus smoking increases the risk of lung cancer by 82.

Question: Have any studies of the people working in midtown during the asbestos snows been made?

Answer: "We did some tests to show the high dissemination of asbestos. No one knows the effect on the people."

32. P. Brodeur, New Yorker, 1968. See also Brodeur, Asbestos and Enzymes (New York: Ballantine Books, 1972); testimony of Selikoff, Executive Session of New York City Council, Environmental Protection Committee, February 25, 1971.

33. Interview with Fabricant, November 1970; interview with Kramer, April 9, 1971; interview with Pieratti, February 24, 1971.

34. La Monica v. Kretchmer, N.Y. Law Journal, November 18, 1970, p. 19, Riccobono, J.

35. Interview, with Kramer, April 9, 1971.

36. Village Voice, April 16, 1970.

37. N.Y.C. Adm. Code, ch. 57, sec. 1403.2-9.11 (b) (1971) and regulations thereunder.

38. Testimony of Selikoff at Executive Session of New York City Council, Environmental Protection Committee, February 25, 1971.

39. Testimony of Harold Romer at Executive Session of New York City Council, Environmental Protection Committee, February 25, 1971.

40. Interview with Romer, January, 1971; testimony of Dr. Irving Selikoff, February 25, 1971.

41. Ibid.

42. Testimony of Selikoff at Executive Session of New York City Council, Environmental Protection Committee, February 25, 1971.

43. Testimony of Executive Session of New York City Council, Environmental Protection Committee, February 25, 1971.

44. Testimony of Selikoff at Executive Session of New York City Council, Environmental Protection Committee, February 25, 1971.

45. Interview with Ferrand, April 21, 1971.

46. Interview with Kramer, April 9, 1971.

47. Citation for emergency powers and procedures.

48. Intradepartmental Quarterly Progress Report, December 31, 1970.

49. On May 4, 1971, the New York Times reported that coats made with 8 percent asbestos cloth imported from Italy had been discontinued as hazardous. Well over 100,000 coats had been sold. An individual who knew he owned such a coat was advised to bury it.

5

This brief New York City case study has sought to illustrate the problems and complexities of implementing traditional air pollution control laws, as well as some of the individual shortcomings in New York City's air pollution control management program.

It is clear from the study that there are no "solutions" that will automatically solve New York City's air problem. However, the study does suggest several policy approaches that are desirable and reasonably effective; it also documents long-standing traditional approaches that either cannot be implemented or, when enforced, appear to have had minimal impact on air quality. In addition, the study illustrates the woefully inadequate allocation of air pollution control resources in the country's major metropolis by local, state, and federal governments.

Certainly tough and enforceable laws are a desirable policy goal. Laws that are not enforceable do more harm than no laws at all, for they merely cloud the issue and confuse reality. New York City's air pollution control laws are certainly tough—the standards are reasonably high and they cover every conceivable pollution source—but these laws are not enforceable if the pollution sources to be controlled are too numerous to allow reasonable management (for example, individual residential and commercial boilers and incinerators). The law also is not enforceable if the city allocates grossly insufficient resources to the enforcement program (as in the case of industrial pollution or licensing programs).

Therefore, it seems clear that New York City must adopt a policy goal of minimizing the number of existing and future individual pollution sources within the city. At the same time the city must increase the number of field and other enforcement personnel in order to bring within manageable proportions the relationship between the number of pollution sources and the number of enforcement personnel.

Minimization of sources can gradually be accomplished through the use of large common facilities instead of individual boilers and incinerators; mandatory functional economies such as total energy systems in new construction; and stringent control of the growth of new polluting activities. A logical corollary of this policy is to conserve energy on a large scale through modification of the structural and other pertinent requirements in the local building code.

Without doubt, the most successful air pollution control law ever enacted by New York City is the one restricting the sulfur content of fuel. This law was manageable because it was aimed at the relatively few fuel distributors early in the distribution chain rather than at the large number of ultimate fuel consumers at the end of the distribution chain. Air monitoring reports gathered by the New York City Air Resources Department indicates that this law has had a substantial positive impact on air quality. (The fact that the sulfur dioxide content of New York City's air does not yet satisfy federal air quality standards should not detract from the fact that the quantity of sulfur dioxide in the air has decreased substantially in most parts of the city.)

The success of the sulfur content law should not be surprising to those who remember what happened after World War II when New York City switched from coal to oil heating. It is a documented fact that this fuel change caused a dramatic long-term decrease in the amount of soot in New York City's air. Since these two fuel changes—from coal to oil and from high sulfur to low sulfur—have had such a positive impact on air quality, New York City should actively pursue a policy to maximize the use of energy sources that are nonpolluting (such as steam) or minimally polluting (such as gas). Undoubtedly, such a policy will not be easy to pursue with rising fuel prises and reported national fuel shortages. However, as a matter of national policy for the protection of public health, large urban centers must be given high priority in the use of low-polluting fuels for both space heating and the generation of energy.

Traditional air pollution control regulatory technique prohibits the emission of a pollutant, such as smoke or particulate matter, into the air if the emission from a particular source exceeds a specified quantity or density. The classic example is New York City's law restricting the emission of smoke for three-quarters of a century. But despite extensive enforcement efforts, the smoke control and other emission laws have failed to control air pollution. The failure of these laws is due primarily to the fact that the nature of the violation precludes systematic control of very large numbers of emission sources. Emission control laws permit the polluter to use the polluting matter (such as coal or oil) and the equipment (boiler or incinerator), provided the emission standard is not exceeded by the polluter. Thus the burden is on the enforcing agency to find and observe the violation, and because nearly all pollutant emissions occur irregularly, systematic inspection systems tend to be time-consuming and haphazard. In addition, such inspections must be repeated regularly and frequently because even good equipment with a control mechanism will pollute unless it is properly maintained and repaired.

Although smoke and other emission laws are inefficient and consequently expensive as a primary means of enforcement, they do have a useful role to play in an air pollution control regulatory scheme. If the pollution sources are of manageable number, such laws can be used as an effective supplementary enforcement technique. They also are useful for agency crackdowns on large polluters such as public utilities and major industries.

But even for supplementary uses, the enforcement of smoke and other emission standards requires an adequate number of inspectors and back-up clerical staff to spot-check pollution sources during the regular working day as well as at night and on weekends and holidays. (Los Angeles' reported "dawn raids" on industrial pollution sources apparently are quite effective.) The full development of scanning and monitoring technology and their required installation undoubtedly will make possible such continuous monitoring.

As New York City long ago recognized, the required licensing of polluting equipment can be a useful technique. It is a preventive program that places the burden on the potential polluter, who must appear before and satisfy the enforcement agency of compliance with the law before a license is issued. Although licensing is a very appealing regulatory technique, New York City's extensive experience with it has illustrated several problems that can easily arise in connection with licensing:

1. The success of any licensing system is entirely dependent upon adequate program funding to provide the substantial bureaucratic staff needed to expeditiously process applications and do equipment check-ups. Without adequate supportive staff, a licensing program is (and in New York City has been) easily ignored.

2. As a practical matter an air pollution licensing program is very difficult and sometimes impossible to enforce. The usual method of enforcement is license withdrawal or suspension—a simple and effective technique. However, illegal air-polluting equipment is rarely shut down because of the social consequences if housing, employment, or electrical power are affected. Thus licensing lacks its usual clout.

3. Programs to require across-the-board licensing of old equipment can be expected to encounter strong resistance from polluters. New York City has attempted to license equipment designed in different time scales—new equipment in new plants, altered equipment in existing plants, and old equipment in existing plants. The first two categories are traditional licensing areas, and such programs generally

encounter little resistance from polluters because the equipment upgrading is required only if the polluter chooses to replace, alter, or
install new equipment. Thus initial decision-making, timing, and
financial planning remain in private hands and are not directly affected
by the enforcing agencies.

The licensing of old equipment in old plants is not traditional,
and represents a major New York City experiment. The program's
limited success in obtaining compliance certainly indicates that wide-
scale mandatory upgrading of old equipment may encounter strong and
persistent resistance from the private as well as governmental sectors,
and therefore as a practical matter may be unenforceable. Some factors
that apparently have played a role in the program's relative failure
are the program's untimely (from the owners' viewpoint) adverse economic effects on persons or governmental bodies too numerous to
easily coerce; New York City's continuing failure to provide sufficient
enforcement and other resources needed for such program; and the
initial failure to provide options and economic incentives (New York
City later helped arrange low-interest loans for landlords to upgrade
boilers and incinerators).

The air pollution control enforcement procedures observed in
New York City were unfortunately woefully inadequate, not only at the
agency level but also at the court level. This study has detailed the
sometimes shocking, archaic, and inefficient conditions in the New
York City criminal courts, which had exclusive jurisdiction over air
pollution enforcement until the fall of 1971, when new legislation gave
the Environmental Control Board limited enforcement power at the
administrative level.

It is to be hoped that the new enforcement agency (the Environmental Control Board) and the new procedures will result in a successful expedition of cases, and hopefully deter polluting activities. With
adequate resources and competent professionals, the administrative
board should meet with reasonable success. However, its work may
be impeded by the fact that the law grants the polluter the unusual
privilege of being entitled upon appeal to a de novo trial at the discretion of the courts, and prohibits counsel for the environmental control
agency from litigating an appealed case before the court on behalf of
the agency (only the city corporation counsel may represent the agency
before a court.) Despite high hopes for the success of the administrative board, its first year and a half of operation were seriously
hampered and finally blocked by the fact that Mayor John V. Lindsay
failed to appoint board members, thus preventing the staff from im-
posing penalties on polluters who already has been tried. Only the
Environmental Control Board has power to impose penalties.

The case studies of industrial pollution, sulfur content of fuels,
and control of asbestos spraying were used to illustrate in a concrete

and detailed fashion some of the problems encountered by New York City in its dealings with the business community. Industrial pollution has never been adequately controlled or given adequate enforcement resources; it has always been a low-priority item. As a result industry continues to pollute despite tough air pollution control laws. In contrast, control of the sulfur content of fuels was given high priority by the federal Department of Health, Education and Welfare (behind the scenes), the city's Air Resources Department, the city corporation counsel, and Mayor Lindsay. This strong leadership, plus the fact that the problem's solution was amenable to efficient low-cost enforcement management, has lead to singular success in controlling the emission of sulfur dioxide. But the asbestos spraying control program lacked strong leadership from the mayor or federal agency, and was the subject of controversy among the city departments and the city corporation counsel because of its dramatic economic effect upon the construction industry. Eventually the spraying of asbestos was prohibited by the city corporation counsel; however, the technique of spraying a substance into the open air in order to fireproof materials was allowed to continue although there was no knowledge about the effect spraying large quantities of an unknown substance into the air would have on the public health.

Air pollution is a low-visibility public health problem with high priority for the relatively healthy citizen only during and immediately after pollution episodes. Nevertheless research indicates that air pollution's low-level long-range effect on urban populations may be very serious. It is the author's hope that this study has illustrated the need for three major components in any successful air pollution control program: (1) manageable laws that can realistically be enforced, (2) the allocation of adequate resources to enforce those laws, and (3) executive leadership of the air pollution control programs at the highest levels. Intermittent leadership and inadequate resources will never do the job.

TABLE A.1

Inspector Activities, 1957-70

Year	Field Man-Days	Patrol Hours	Court Hours	Training Hours	Miscellaneous Hours	Office Hours
1957	5,323.79	6,341.8	4.38	n.a.	n.a.	n.a.
1958	5,300	7,802.6	4.46	n.a.	n.a.	n.a.
1959	5,049	5,232	5.24	n.a.	n.a.	n.a.
1960	5,043.6	2,248.5	5.93	n.a.	n.a.	n.a.
1961	6,275.3	2,352.1	5.24	n.a.	n.a.	n.a.
1962	7,214	12,836.	4.76	n.a.	n.a.	n.a.
1963	6,801.4	12,515.	5.00	n.a.	n.a.	n.a.
1964	6,690.1	11,495.8	5.1	n.a.	n.a.	n.a.
1965	5,947.6	9,748.8	6.2	n.a.	n.a.	n.a.
1966	4,733.8	16,045.9	4,406.6	n.a.	n.a.	n.a.
1967	n.a.	n.a.	n.a.	n.a.	n.a.	n.a.
1968	n.a.	n.a.	n.a.	n.a.	n.a.	n.a.
1969	n.a.	n.a.	n.a.	n.a.	n.a.	n.a.
1970	40,706	n.a.	6,504	7,543	3,482	37,586

TABLE A.2

Inspector Work and Leave Hours, 1970

1970	Work Hours	Leave Hours
January	10,465.0	2,180.0
February	7,986.2	1,992.0
March	8,962.2	1,588.0
April	8,957.0	1,685.0
May	8,385.0	1,492.0
June	7,716.0	1,941.5
July	5,051.5	2,831.0
August	5,531.5	2,307.5
September	7,073.7	1,608.5
October	7,075.5	2,250.0
November	6,543.0	2,654.5
December	8,574.5	1,901.5
Total	98,621.0	24,431.

Note: This table gives an indication of the difference between budgeted time and working time.

TABLE A.3

Citizen Complaints, 1957–70

Year	Number Received	Number Inspected	Number Resulting in No Action	Number Resulting in Violation Notice	Number Resulting in Summonses
1957	15,500	15,865	15,168	2,196	371
1958	14,293	12,949	11,377	2,962	513
1959	17,185	15,597	12,925	2,502	347
1960	15,615	14,467	11,116	1,988	297
1961	19,534	17,565	14,026	2,284	374
1962	20,328	18,452	14,412	2,238	446
1963	19,906	18,673	14,434	1,688	857
1964	24,408	20,997	16,304	1,581	687
1965	32,002	23,260	18,960	1,108	656
1966	22,668	11,326	8,637	768	n.a.
1967	44,120	n.a.	n.a.	n.a.	n.a.
1968	31,992	n.a.	n.a.	n.a.	n.a.
1969	31,606	n.a.	n.a.	30	n.a.
1970	34,138	10,672	8,140	836	2,767

TABLE A.4

Inspections, by Origin or Cause, 1957-70

Year	Citizen Complaint Origin	Patrol Origin	Reinspection	Permit Application	Miscellaneous	Total
1957	15,865	2,567	2,346	n.a.	1,968	23,346 (22,746?)
1958	12,949	3,475	6,360	n.a.	1,123	23,907
1959	15,597	2,849	5,750	n.a.	2,296	26,492
1960	14,467	2,285	5,538	n.a.	7,622	29,917
1961	17,565	2,658	6,770	3,463	2,446	32,902
1962	18,452	2,679	8,959	1,352	2,809	34,251
1963	18,673	2,545	8,497	887	2,840	32,342
1964	20,997	2,268	7,725	908	2,433	34,324
1965	23,260	1,764	6,300	1,177	1,738	34,239
1966	11,326	3,041	3,212	591	1,073	12,110
1967						
1968						
1969						
1970	10,672	3,603	519	n.a.	4,949	19,657

95

TABLE A.5

Inspections, by Resulting Action 1957-70

Year	Total Number of Inspections	No Action	Violation Notice	Summons
1957	23,346	17,514	2,704	560
1958	23,907	17,737	4,293	754
1959	26,492	18,675	4,943	578
1960	29,917	16,654	5,077	559
1961	32,902	20,796	5,444	753
1962	34,251	23,371	5,939	780
1963	32,342	22,931	5,467	1,317[c]
1964	34,324	24,029	5,806	1,147
1965	34,239	25,260	4,879	1,185
1966[a]	12,110	11,849	2,750	1,077
1967	27,329	n.a.	5,016	1,682
1968	32,761	n.a.	8,236	2,904
1969	40,627	n.a.	30,501[b]	4,334[d]
1970	20,014 (19,638)	8,659	9,135	4,303[d]

[a] The table shows corrected 1966 figures for the number of inspections and summonses. It is said that the figures originally distributed were inflated by personnel, since dismissed, who under pressure to produce, undertook to give the commissioner results, whether true or not. The original figures were 19,243 inspections, and 2,971 summonses.

[b] The number of violation notices rose dramatically in 1969 and then dropped again because in 1969 the Department undertook a huge mailing of notices that produced a low response.

[c] It is not clear why there was a sharp rise in summonses in 1963.

[d] The numbers of summonses served in 1969 and 1970 are considerably higher than in the past because about half the summonses served were for failure to apply for an upgrading permit under Local Law 14. In 1969, of 4,334 summonses, 2,700 were Local Law 14; in 1968, of 2,904 summonses, only 800 were Local Law. Previously, Local Law 14 summonses were served only after physical examination of the equipment, not just on the basis of the record. In addition, Local Law 14 permitted the service of per diem violations. Thus, as many summonses as days of violation could be served on the same piece of equipment.

TABLE A.6

Inspections, By Resulting Action and Origin, 1957-70

Year	No Action Citizen Complaint Origin	No Action Reinspection	Violation Notice Citizen Complaint Origin	Violation Notice Patrol Origin	Summons Citizen Complaint Origin	Summons Patrol Origin	Total Inspections	Total Summonses
1957	15,168	2,346	2,196	508	371	189	23,346	560
1958	11,377	6,360	2,962	1,331	513	241	23,907	754
1959	12,925	5,750	2,502	2,441	347	231	26,492	578
1960	11,116	5,538	1,988	3,089	297	262	29,917	559
1961	14,026	6,770	2,284	3,160	374	379	32,902	753
1962	14,412	8,959	2,233	3,706	446	334	34,251	780
1963	14,434	8,497	1,688	3,779	857	460	32,342	1,317
1964	16,304	7,725	1,581	4,225	687	461	34,324	1,147
1965	18,960	6,300	1,108	3,771	656	529	34,239	1,185
1966	8,637	3,212	768	1,986	2,273	703	12,110	1,077
1967	n.a.		5,016		1,682		27,329	1,682
1968	n.a.		8,236		2,904		32,761	2,904
1969	n.a.		30	501	4,334		40,627	4,334
1970	8,140	519	836	1,368	2,767	1,164	20,014	4,303

97

TABLE A.7

Disposition of Air Pollution Control Cases by Criminal Court

Year	Total Number of Cases Pending Before Court	Number of Cases Fined	Number of Cases Withdrawn by City	Number of Cases Dismissed by Court	Number of Suspended Sentences
1956	360	304	4	8	44
1957	601	470	8	17	106
1958	693	498	11	27	157
1959	592	472	12	20	88
1960	704	566	12	17	109
1961	685	606	8	27	44
1962	683	620	10	14	39
1963	1,254	1,123	22	33	76
1964	1,088	1,004	10	38	36
1965	1,070	997	12	32	29
1966	2,774	2,647	19	61	47
1967	1,372	1,296	12	34	30
1968					
1969					
1970	12,619	2,702	282	325	?

The information in this book was obtained in part from interviews with the following persons, all of whom I wish to thank for their
time and cooperation (all titles dated are as of the interview date).

NEW YORK CITY AIR RESOURCES DEPARTMENT

Joseph Coffrini, Assistant Court Officer
Dr. Edward Ferrand, Director of Technical Services
Fred C. Hart, Deputy Commissioner
Louis Leibowitz, Director of Enforcement Bureau
Alex Mautner, Assistant in Automotive Division
Alfred Pieratti, Executive Director of Engineering and Enforcement
Benjamin C. Radzka, Director of Industrial Processes Task Force
Harold Romer, Assistant Commissioner
Joseph Schechter, Director of Bureau of Enforcement

THE FOLLOWING PERSONS WERE FORMERLY WITH
THE AIR RESOURCES DEPARTMENT

May Dorfman, former Executive Assistant to the Commissioner
Jack Fensterstock, former Director of Program and Planning
Austin Heller, former Commissioner
Simon Mencher, former Deputy Commissioner
Robert N. Rickles, former Commissioner
Ellsworth Roberts, former Chief Inspector and Court Officer
Conrad Simon, former Assistant Commissioner

NEW YORK CITY ENVIRONMENTAL PROTECTION
ADMINISTRATION - OFFICE OF GENERAL COUNSEL

At the time of this writing, the General Counsel and the two
attorneys assigned to air resources had resigned. As a result, all
persons listed below are formerly with EPA.
Neil Fabricant, Esq., former General Counsel
Robert Czeisler, Esq., former Assistant General Counsel assigned
to Air Resources

John Kaufman, Esq., former Assistant General Counsel assigned to
Air Resources

Douglas J. Kramer, Esq., former Assistant General Counsel assigned
to Air Resources

Steven Salup, Esq., former Assistant General Counsel assigned to
Air Resources

NEW YORK CITY CORPORATION COUNSEL

Norman Redlich, Esq., First Assistant Corporation Counsel

James Brachman, Esq., former Assistant Corporation Counsel,
Assistant Chief Penalties Division

Joseph M. Callahan, Jr., Esq., Assistant Corporation Counsel, Penalties Division, assigned to Criminal Court, Manhattan, Part 6

Irving Gerstein, Esq., Assistant Corporation Counsel, Chief of Penalties Division

Judith Grad, Esq., Assistant Corporation Counsel, Division of Opinions
and Legislation (helped prepare Freedom to Breathe, Report on
Mayor's Task Force on Air Pollution in the City of New York,
1966) and a legal adviser to the Department in 1967-68.

Eugene Margolis, Esq., Assistant Corporation Counsel, Chief of
Consumer Protection Division (handled Storm King case and city's
antitrust suit against the auto companies charging a conspired
failure to develop auto antipollution devices).

Milton Weinberg, Esq., Assistant Corporation Counsel in Charge of
the Division of Special Legal Assignments (assigned to Oriental
Blvd. case and Plymouth Rock Fuel Corp. case).

Edward Walla, Esq., Assistant Corporation Counsel, Division of
Special Legal Assignments (assistant to Weinberg on Oriental Blvd.
and Plymouth Rock cases)

ASSISTANTS TO MAYOR LINDSAY

Steven Isenberg, Assistant to Mayor
John Berenyi, Assistant to Mayor

CITY COUNCIL

Eldon Clingan, member of Environmental Protection Committee
(interviewed when he was Director of Citizens for Clean Air)

Robert Low, Esq., former Councilman and Chairman of Special Committee to Investigate Air Pollution, "author" of Local Law 14

100

Theodore Weiss, Esq., Chairman of Environmental Protection Committee

NEW YORK STATE DEPARTMENT OF
ENVIRONMENTAL CONSERVATION

Harry H. Hovey, Jr., Associate Director Department of Resources (Albany Office)

Arnold Risman, Associate Air Pollution Control Engineer (N.Y.C. officer in charge of air pollution control)

U.S. ENVIRONMENTAL PROTECTION AGENCY

William S. Baker, Acting Assistant Regional Air Pollution Control Director for Program Development (N.Y.C. office)

Saul J. Harris, Regional Representative, Radiological Health (N.Y.C. office)

Kenneth L. Johnson, Regional Air Pollution Control Director (N.Y.C. office)

William F. Johnson, Esq., Adviser to Compliance Officer (Washington, D.C.)

Dr. Robert S. Kirk, Chief of the Evaluation and Analysis Section (Washington, D.C.)

William H. Megonnell, Compliance Officer and former Regional Air Pollution Control Director in N.Y.C. (Washington, D.C.)

BUSINESS AND CIVIC

Samuel Ashkenazi, former editorial writer with the American Petroleum Institute

Arnold Gubrud, Deputy Director of the Committee for Air and Water Conservation, American Petroleum Institute.

John Keegan, Esq., General Counsel, Consolidated Edison

Don Pattison, Vice President, Model Roland Co. (security analyst specializing in pollution control)

Kenneth Kowald, former Executive Director, New York State Administration for Clean Air Committee

The N.Y.C. materials are also based in part of conversations, some over a period of years, with the following persons:

NEW YORK CITY AIR RESOURCES DEPARTMENT

Arthur Benline, former Commissioner
Richard A. Wolff, former Assistant Commissioner
M. M. Braverman, former Bureau Director (laboratory)
Leo P. Flood, former Bureau Director (engineering)
Harold Glicksman, former Bureau Director (inspectors)
Ralph O'Donoghue, Esq., former departmental legal adviser

OTHER GOVERNMENTAL AGENCIES

Charles Ahlers, formerly in charge of public relations for N.Y.C.
Environmental Protection Administration
Dorothy Banks, former secretary to the Administrator (Eisenbud and
Kretchmer) of the N.Y.C. Environmental Protection Administration
George W. Walsh, Acting Assistant Director for Planning, U.S. Environmental Protection Agency

particulate emmission, 4-68-69
particulates, airborne, 5

recorderes, proper use required, 6
Ringelman chart, 4

soot blowing, 7
sealing, 20-21
smoke, violations, 43
smoke, alarm or air contaminant
  detection, 6
stack tests, 4

sulfur, combined with particulates,
  68-69; content of fuel, 7-8, 68-
  72; control and enforcement, 69-
  70; impact on air, 70-71
summonses, type of violations, 35

upgrading of incinerators and
  boilers, 6

violation, notices informal warnings, 6

ABOUT THE AUTHOR

ESTHER RODITTI SCHACHTER is a Program Officer in the Government and Law, National Affairs Division of the Ford Foundation. Before coming to the Ford Foundation, she was a Senior Research Associate with the Center for Policy Research.

Her interest and involvement in environmental affairs dates back to the early 1960s when, as Assistant Director to the Columbia University Legislative Drafting Research Fund, she headed a project to draft a model air pollution control code for New York City. Since that time she acted as an environmental law consultant to the New York City Air Pollution Control Department; the New School for Social Research—Center for New York City Affairs; the United Nations Association; the Rand Institute; and private consulting firms. She has also taught environmental law at the New School for Social Research, Center for New York City Affairs, and is the author of a number of articles on the subject. She is co-author of Charities and Charitable Foundations, which will be published in fall 1973.

A graduate of the Harvard Law School, Dr. Schachter received her B.A. Magna Cum Laude from the University of California at Los Angeles, where she was Phi Beta Kappa.

DEMONSTRATION DEMOCRACY
(Gordon and Breach, 1971)

> Amitai Etzioni

TECHNOLOGICAL SHORTCUTS TO SOCIAL CHANGE
(Russell Sage Foundation, 1973)

> Amitai Etzioni and Richard Remp

HOSPITAL EFFICIENCY AND PUBLIC POLICY
(Praeger Publishers, 1973)

> Harry I. Greenfield

THE ILLUSION OF EQUALITY:
The Effect of Education on Opportunity, Inequality, and Conflict
(Jossey-Bass, 1972)

> Murray Milner

AIR QUALITY MANAGEMENT AND LAND USE
PLANNING

George Hagevik

STATE ENVIRONMENTAL MANAGEMENT:
Case Studies of Nine States

Elizabeth H. Haskell and Victoria S.
Price

THE ECONOMICS OF AIRBORNE EMISSIONS:
The Case for an Air Rights Market

Douglas R. Mackintosh

ENVIRONMENTAL POLICY: Concepts and
International Implications

Edited by Albert E. Utton and Daniel
H. Henning